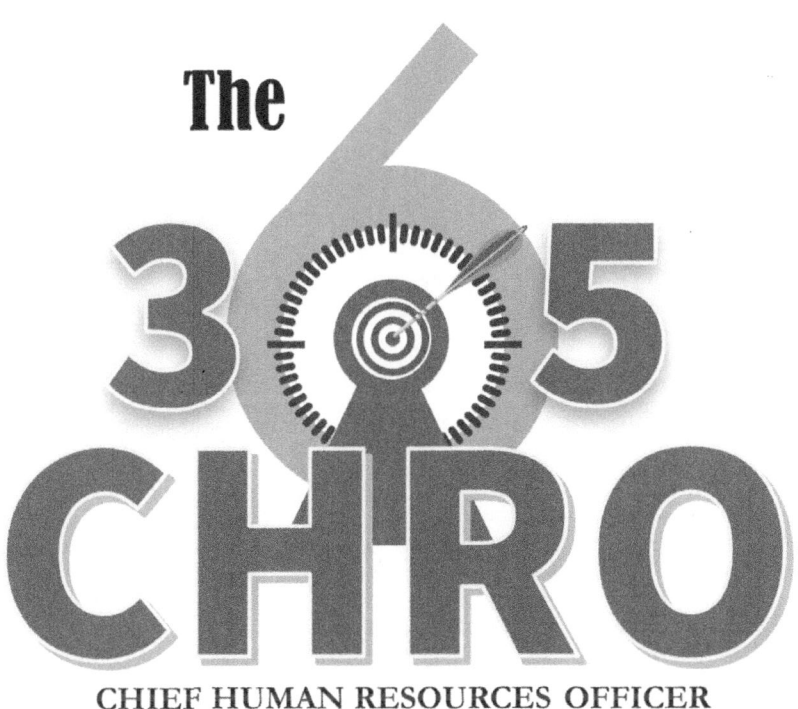

The 365

CHRO

CHIEF HUMAN RESOURCES OFFICER

Elevate Your Leadership with Strategic HR Planning
Unlock the Power of Strategic Thinking to Win the Game

ROB KOCZO

First paperback edition February 2024.

DEDICATION

To those who blazed the trail ahead of me and to those who will follow the road less traveled.

For my Mom and Dad who blazed the trail and sacrificed so much to ensure I would have an opportunity to make a difference. Thank you.

For Beth, Abby, and Jake, who have been next to me and provided unconditional support on the road since day 1. Thank you.

Finally, to my **#1** - thank you for handing me the flashlight and always guiding me through all the trails, and for always being my **#1.**

ACCOLADES

"Every solid game plan requires the right mix of strategy, tactics, innovation, execution, and leadership. Rob Koczo's new book lays out a detailed plan, mixing the right elements needed to influence and impact your organization – taking your winning team to super performance levels in the quickest way possible. The 3-month plan takes a truly systemic view of what's necessary to make every "play" land for you, your team, and your business! Highly recommend reading this valuable resource, for any new CHRO, or seasoned leader looking for a great new playbook."

Donna Latin
ICF Professionally Certified Team Coach

"I observed Rob successfully integrate many of the concepts found in The 365 CHRO into his daily approach while supporting me. The 365 CHRO can be used as a "Pregame Checklist" for any CHRO starting their journey, or as a review for any tenured CHRO who needs a fresh start."

Tammy Mallaise'
Senior Vice President, People & Culture, Zachry

"Rob's approach to The 365 CHRO is something I experienced when he supported me. I recommend Rob's book to anyone starting their journey as CHRO or to anyone needing a refresher on key strategic steps to follow that yield immediate impact."

Leah Kasparek
VP, CHRO, Cameron LNG

"Rob is a seasoned HR expert. I witnessed his precision in implementing the strategies in The 365 CHRO as his colleague and COO. The outcomes were amazing! I highly recommend this playbook for any new CHRO on a mission to quickly add value."

Liza Kapica
Chief Operating Officer, FSP

CONTENTS

CONTENTS

Welcome to Human Resources Stadium—where strategy, agility, value, execution, and teamwork are the benchmarks of success. You're not just stepping into the game of Chief Human Resources Officer (CHRO) leadership; you're gearing up for a championship season that will redefine your success in the first 365 days on the field.

In football, the first quarter sets the tone for the entire game. Similarly, the first 3 months of your leadership will require a well-executed drive leading to a touchdown. This book can serve as a play sheet, including winning plays, strategic moves, and tactical maneuvers to support your success. During your first 3 months, it's important to get a fast start to represent value and your leadership abilities.

If you are taking the CHRO role for the first time, this book will provide a strategic view of assessing your new organization, identifying high-priority items that need to be addressed, and methods to address these problems. Just as a football coach has the play sheet in his hands during the entire game, this book can serve as a reference for strategic and tactical plays to call during your first three months, and subsequently, all 365 days of the year.

If you are an experienced CHRO, this book can directionally provide you with the guidance to call the right plays to identify and solve organizational problems.

As you take the field with your new team as the newly appointed CHRO, you are the star quarterback, the general manager, the offensive and defensive coordinator, and the special teams coach—all combined into one. You'll find insights into the importance of connecting with your teammates—your C Suite leaders, the HR team, and the entire organization. It's time to call the right plays and lay the groundwork for a winning season.

The game has a rulebook, and in HR, compliance is your primary objective. Each year updates are made, helping guide you in the field of regulations and keep your team free from penalties. Think of it as your game's referee, ensuring fair play and protecting your team from unnecessary flags.

Football is dynamic, and so is HR leadership. With this book, I hope to provide helpful tactics to support the fast break moments that can serve as quick wins to change the momentum of the game. It's about seizing opportunities, calling informed plays, and scoring points early in the game.

As you progress through each quarter of the game, chapter by chapter, strategic and tactical play guidance is highlighted to elevate your team to championship status. It's about assembling an all-star lineup, nurturing talent, and creating an environment where everyone can bring their A-game. This book's approach emphasizes building a "fit" organization, founded on principles of engagement, collaboration, partnership, and a culture of inclusion, ensuring that every member feels valued and empowered to contribute their best.

During the game, communication is the key to a well-executed play. The importance of effective communication is critical, not just within your team but across the entire organization. It's time to inspire your players and ensure everyone is on the same page for a winning season.

As you reach the final quarter, you'll be equipped with strategies to sustain a 365-day season—a game plan that assesses past performance and integrates future improvements with organizational goals. This isn't just about winning a single game; it's about securing the championship, season after season.

If you are a first-time CHRO, the plays covered in each chapter are summarized (at the end of Chapter 8) into a non-prescriptive 3-month strategic roadmap to help you score a touchdown quickly. So, here's to you, the CHRO—the quarterback, coach, general manager, offensive and defensive coordinator, and special teams coach. As you have picked up by now, I am a fan of football, as evident from the metaphors throughout this opening.

In most cases, I believe football contains a common language that we can all appreciate as we have either cheered our high-school or college team, our kids, or family members who have played the sport, or simply watched a college or NFL game on the weekend.

Football also serves as a great example of unifying star talent, connecting people from diverse backgrounds through the excitement and passion for achieving common goals.

Throughout this book, simple football analogies will be provided to illustrate key concepts and make them more relatable, regardless of your familiarity with the sport.

Supporting Game Day Context

As most human resources organizations manage various functions, from talent acquisition and recruitment to compliance and strategic planning, remember that each play is crucial to achieving success. Just as every player has a specific role to play, each HR function contributes to the overall effectiveness of the team.

Talent Acquisition and Recruitment:

Attracting, sourcing, and hiring qualified candidates to fill vacant positions within the organization. This involves developing recruitment strategies, posting job openings, screening resumes, conducting interviews, and making hiring decisions.

Employee Onboarding and Orientation:

The process of integrating new employees into the organization through comprehensive onboarding and orientation programs. This includes providing new hires with essential information about company policies, procedures, benefits, and culture to help them acclimate to their roles and the organization.

Employee Relations:

Proactively managing relationships between employees and the organization. This involves addressing employee concerns, resolving conflicts, and promoting a positive work environment conducive to collaboration, productivity, and morale.

Performance Management:

Overseeing the performance management processes, including goal setting, performance evaluations, feedback, and performance improvement plans. This involves providing support and guidance to managers and employees to ensure alignment with organizational goals and expectations.

Training and Development:

Designing and implementing training and development

programs to enhance employee skills, knowledge, and capabilities. This includes identifying training needs, designing curriculum, facilitating training sessions, and evaluating training effectiveness to support employee growth and career advancement.

Compensation and Benefits Administration:

Managing the compensation and benefits programs to attract, retain, and motivate employees. This includes conducting salary surveys, establishing pay structures, administering employee benefits such as health insurance, retirement plans, and leave policies, and ensuring compliance with relevant laws and regulations.

Employee Engagement and Retention:

Fostering employee engagement and retention through initiatives aimed at enhancing job satisfaction, motivation, and commitment. This includes conducting employee surveys, organizing events and activities, and implementing recognition and reward programs to promote a positive workplace culture.

HR Information Systems (HRIS) Management:

Technology that is used to streamline HR processes and manage employee data. This includes implementing and maintaining HRIS platforms, managing employee records, generating reports, and ensuring data accuracy and security.

Compliance and Legal Requirements:

Ensuring compliance with employment laws, regulations, and company policies to mitigate legal risks and promote fairness and equity in the workplace. This includes staying informed about changes in labor laws, conducting audits, and addressing compliance issues.

Payroll Management:

In many organizations, payroll management is another critical function of the HR team. HR oversees the processing of payroll, including calculating wages, deducting taxes and other withholdings, and distributing paychecks or facilitating direct deposits.

HR manages payroll records and compliance with wage and hour laws (i.e. Davis Bacon. Overtime, etc.) to prevent potential legal issues. (If your organization is not responsible for payroll management, the function typically resides within the accounting function).

Strategic Planning and Organizational Development:

Partnering with senior leadership to align HR strategies with overall business objectives and drive organizational effectiveness and growth. This involves identifying talent gaps, succession planning, workforce planning, and implementing initiatives to support organizational change and transformation.

Other Supporting Game Day Context

Lean Six Sigma Tools:

1. **Value Stream Mapping (VSM)**: Used to visualize and analyze the flow and helps identify areas of waste and opportunities for improvement.

2. **Kaizen Events**: Short-term improvement projects focused on rapidly changing specific processes. They involve cross-functional teams working together to solve problems and implement solutions quickly.

3. **5S Methodology**: A systematic approach to workplace organization aimed at creating a clean, orderly, and efficient work environment.

4. **Root Cause Analysis (RCA)**: A method for identifying the underlying causes of problems or defects. It involves asking "why" multiple times to uncover the root cause, rather than just addressing symptoms.

5. **Pareto Analysis**: Also known as the 80/20 rule, is used to prioritize improvement efforts by identifying the most significant contributors to a problem.

6. **Failure Mode and Effects Analysis (FMEA)**: A proactive risk assessment tool used to identify potential failures in a process and their potential effects.

7. **Control Charts**: Used to monitor process performance over time and detect any significant changes or deviations from the norm.

Change Management Tools:

1. **Stakeholder Analysis**: Helps identify and assess the impact of change and categorizes stakeholders based on their level of influence and interest in the change initiative.

2. **Change Impact Assessment**: Evaluate the potential effects of a proposed change on different aspects of the organization.

3. **Communication Plan**: Outlines how information about the change will be communicated to stakeholders. process.

4. **Training and Development Programs**: Provide employees with the knowledge, skills, and resources they need to adapt to change successfully.

5. **Resistance Management**: Helps identify and address resistance to change among employees.

6. **Change Readiness Assessment**: Evaluate the organization's readiness for change by assessing factors such as leadership support, employee readiness, and organizational culture.

Project Management Tools:

1. **Gantt Charts**: Visual representations of project schedules that display tasks, timelines, dependencies, and milestones.

2. **Kanban Boards**: Visual task management tools that use columns and cards to represent work stages and progress.

3. **Collaboration Tools:** Allow for real-time messaging, file sharing, video conferencing, and project discussions, enhancing teamwork and coordination.

4. **Risk Management Tools:** Help teams identify, assess, prioritize, and mitigate project risks.

5. **Issue Tracking Tools:** Help teams manage and resolve project issues.

6. **Resource Planning Tools:** Allocate and manage project resources effectively. They provide visibility into resource availability, workload, and utilization, facilitating resource allocation and capacity planning.

7. **Reporting and Analytics Tools:** Help teams analyze project data, track key performance indicators (KPIs), and generate insightful reports. They enable data-driven decision-making and performance monitoring.

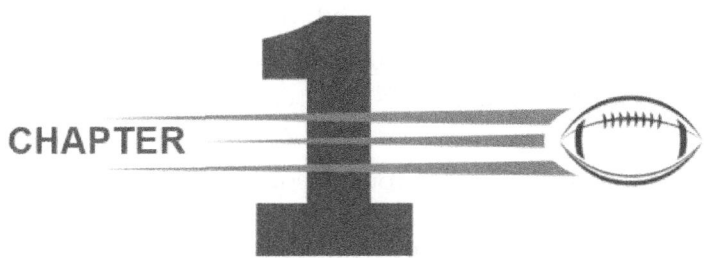

CHAPTER 1

Crafting Your Playbook

✓ Visionary Leadership – Setting the Stage for Success
✓ The Offensive Strategy – Driving HR Success with Precision Plays
✓ Defensive Resilience – Fortifying HR Strategies for Organizational Stability
✓ Special Teams Excellence – Maximizing HR Impact through Strategic Collaboration
✓ The Hall of Fame Mindset – Elevating HR Leadership through Valuable Contributions

Visionary Leadership - Setting the Stage for Success

Visionary leaders are the architects of crafting a path to victory. As you step into the role of the Chief Human Resources Officer (CHRO), envision yourself as the head coach, charting the course for success in the stadium of human resources.

Before the opening kickoff of this chapter, I'd like to start with the inspirational words of legendary football coach Vince Lombardi: "Leaders aren't born, they are made. And they are made just like anything else, through hard work." This sets the tone of visionary leadership, where strategic planning and a forward-thinking mindset become the first down markers of your season.

Visionary leadership is not about predicting the future but rather creating it. Just as a football coach develops a winning game plan, you'll need to craft a strategic and tactical playbook that aligns HR initiatives with the broader organizational goals. The opening of this chapter serves as the motivational pep talk before the big game, confirming that you are the star player brought in to shape the future of the entire organization.

Survey the Field: Gaining a Deep Understanding

As you step into the role of CHRO, your first task is to survey the field of HR within your organization. You'll need to understand the uniqueness of the team and organization, like a quarterback taking the field before the game to assess field conditions.

Tactical Play:

- Conduct a comprehensive analysis of your current HR organization, industry landscape and trends, and emerging challenges.
- Identify key pain points that are considered a top priority to address.

- Identify key players in the HR stadium, both within and outside your organization.
- Evaluate existing technologies supporting current HR processes and overall employee expectations.

Crafting a Vision - A Strategic Blueprint

With insights from your scan, it's time to assemble the data to begin crafting version 1 of a high-level hypothesis of your team. As the head coach, you'll need to develop the plays that not only guide your team through the current game but also anticipate future opponents and strategies for the entire season.

Tactical Play:

- Engage in strategic conversations with organizational leaders to align HR initiatives with broader organizational goals.
- Envision the ideal state of HR of your organization in the current year and for future seasons.
- Define key performance indicators (KPIs) that will measure the success of your initiatives and provide fact-based data to support future adjustments.

Communicating the Vision - Inspiring Your Team

Effectively communicating the vision is critical. Your ability to articulate the vision will provide clarity and direction to the team, ensuring alignment, facilitating collaboration, and synergy, in working towards shared objectives for the game, the season, and for seasons to come. Moreover, the CHRO will inspire the team, much like a coach motivating players before a game.

Tactical Play:

- Develop a clear and concise narrative that communicates the vision in a way that resonates with your team(s).
- Use storytelling techniques to make the vision relatable and memorable.

- Foster an open communication culture where team members can provide feedback and contribute to the realization of the vision.

Flexibility and Adaptability - Navigating Changes

HR leadership is not about strict adherence to a plan; it's about being flexible and agile. By embracing flexibility, you'll be positioned to tailor strategies and initiatives to address emerging challenges and seize new opportunities, ensuring the sustained effectiveness of the HR function. Just as a seasoned quarterback will call an audible at the line of scrimmage to adjust a play, a flexible CHRO needs to navigate these types of changes as they arise.

Tactical Play:

- Build flexibility (and contingencies for timing) into your vision to accommodate unforeseen challenges and opportunities.
- Establish feedback loops to continually assess the effectiveness of the vision and adjust as needed.
- Encourage a culture of innovation and learning, where the HR team is empowered to adapt to changing circumstances.

Your role is not just about managing the current state, but also shaping the future. As you progress, you'll need to translate the vision into actionable plays, ensuring that your team executes the game plan with precision and purpose. Translating vision into actionable plays involves breaking down overarching goals into tactical plays that team members can understand and execute. This process requires aligning individual tasks with the broader vision, ensuring that each action contributes meaningfully to the organization's objectives.

The Offensive Strategy - Driving HR Success with Precision Plays

The HR strategy serves as the playbook, where every play is calculated to support achieving organizational goals. The great Super Bowl-winning coach of the Dallas Cowboys Coach, Tom Landry once said, "Setting a goal is not the main thing. It is deciding how you will go about achieving it and staying with that plan." Embrace the offensive strategy, and let each calculated move bring your HR team closer to scoring points for the entire organization.

Understanding Offensive Dynamics: A Strategic Overview

A football team plans and executes an offensive plan geared against the opponent to win the game. HR also needs a tactical plan to drive organizational success. Picture your HR team as the cohesive unit executing plays to achieve your strategic objectives.

Tactical Play:

- **Goal Setting:** Clearly define HR goals aligned with organizational objectives. These could include talent acquisition, employee engagement, or diversity and inclusion initiatives.
- **Resource Allocation:** Strategically allocate resources (to include technology improvements) to support offensive plays. Consider this as assigning players to positions on the field.
- **Performance Metrics:** Establish KPIs to measure the success of offensive HR initiatives.

Talent Acquisition - Scoring Key Players

An effective offensive strategy begins with acquiring top talent—your star players. Just as a football team scouts for skilled athletes, HR must attract and recruit individuals who align with the organization's vision and goals.

Tactical Play:

- **Strategic Recruitment:** Develop a recruitment strategy that targets those with the skills and values that are important for organizational success.
- **Employer Branding:** Enhance the organization's employer brand to attract top talent.
- **Onboarding Excellence:** Ensure a seamless onboarding process to integrate new hires into the team effectively.

Employee Engagement - Sustaining Momentum

The offensive strategy doesn't end with recruitment; it extends to keeping the existing team engaged and motivated. Keeping the existing team engaged and motivated involves fostering a positive work environment where employees feel valued, recognized, and challenged. Implementing regular feedback mechanisms and recognition programs can boost morale and reinforce a sense of accomplishment. Additionally, providing opportunities for skill development and career growth demonstrates a commitment to employee success, further enhancing motivation and retention. Think of it as maintaining momentum throughout the game to sustain a successful drive down the field.

Tactical Play:

- **Communication Channels:** Establish effective communication channels to keep employees informed and engaged.
- **Recognition and Rewards:** Implement a rewards system to acknowledge and celebrate individual and team achievements.
- **Professional Development:** Provide opportunities for skill development and career growth, coaching players to enhance their capabilities.

Diversity and Inclusion - Building a Versatile Lineup

Just as a diverse lineup gives a football team versatility and adaptability, a diverse and inclusive workforce enhances organizational resilience and creativity. Diversity and inclusion are crucial for fostering innovation, creativity, and resilience within the team. Embracing diverse perspectives and experiences not only enriches decision-making processes but also cultivates a culture of respect and belonging where every individual feels empowered to contribute their unique talents and insights.

Tactical Play:

- **Inclusive Recruitment:** Actively promote diversity in recruitment efforts.
- **Training and Awareness:** Conduct diversity and inclusion training to foster a culture of acceptance and understanding.
- **Inclusive Policies:** Implement policies that support diversity and inclusion, creating an environment where every team member feels valued.

HR Technology - Leveraging Cutting-Edge Tools

An effective offensive strategy leverages tools and technologies to enhance performance. In HR, this translates to adopting and optimizing processes using Human Resources Information Systems (HRIS), analytics tools, and other technologies. HRIS technologies streamline administrative tasks, allowing HR professionals to focus more on strategic initiatives that boost team performance. By centralizing employee data and automating processes like payroll and performance management, HRIS platforms provide timely insights and support informed decision-making, ultimately enabling teams to operate more efficiently and effectively. Additionally, features such as self-service portals empower employees to access information and resources independently, fostering a culture of autonomy and accountability within the team.

Tactical Play:

- **Technology Assessment:** Evaluate the existing HR technology stack and identify areas for enhancement.

- **Opportunity:** Introduce new technologies to streamline HR processes, enhancing efficiency and effectiveness.

- **Data-Driven Decision-Making:** Encourage a culture of data-driven decision-making, like a football team using analytics to refine their game plan.

Continuous Improvement - Adjusting the Playbook

Successful football teams adapt their offensive strategies based on the opposing defense. Similarly, HR must be agile, continuously refining its playbook to align with organizational goals and external factors. Continuous improvement is a cornerstone of organizational success, driving ongoing innovation and evolution. By fostering a culture that embraces feedback, iteration, and learning from both successes and failures, businesses can adapt to changing market dynamics and stay ahead of the competition.

Tactical Play:

- **Feedback Loops:** Establish feedback mechanisms to gather insights from employees and stakeholders.

- **Regular Evaluation:** Periodically evaluate the effectiveness of HR strategies and adjust as needed.

- **Agile Mindset:** Cultivate an agile mindset within the HR team, encouraging adaptability in response to evolving challenges.

As you craft and implement your offensive HR strategy, remember that success lies not just in individual plays but in the seamless integration of the entire offensive playbook.

Defensive Resilience - Fortifying HR Strategies for Organizational Stability

In the game of HR leadership, defensive resilience is the shield that safeguards organizational stability. Picture yourself as the right guard protecting the quarterback, standing firm against external pressures and internal disruptions. Vince Lombardi, head football coach of the Green Bay Packers and winner of five NFL championships said it best: "It's not whether you get knocked down, it's whether you get up."

This section unfolds like a defensive playbook, guiding you through firming up HR strategies to weather storms and emerge stronger. Your defensive resilience in HR will uphold the integrity and stability of the entire organization.

Defensive Alignment: Strengthening HR Foundations

Much like a solid defense in football forms the backbone of a team, HR's defensive resilience is crucial for maintaining stability within the organization.

Strengthening HR foundations is essential for safeguarding organizational integrity and mitigating legal and operational risks. By regularly evaluating and updating policies, ensuring adherence to regulatory requirements, and proactively identifying potential risks, HR can establish a solid framework that supports sustainable growth and fosters a culture of trust and accountability within the organization.

Tactical Play:

- **Policies:** Review and strengthen HR policies to ensure they align with current legal standards and industry best practices.
- **Compliance:** Establish a compliance monitoring system to stay ahead of changes in employment laws and regulations.
- **Risk Assessment:** Conduct a thorough risk assessment to identify potential vulnerabilities in HR processes.

Crisis Management - Responding to Unexpected Plays

A resilient football defense responds quickly to unexpected offensive audibles on the field. Similarly, HR must be equipped to handle crises with agility and composure. In HR, responding to the unexpected requires agility, empathy, and strategic thinking to navigate unforeseen challenges. By proactively planning, communicating, and implementing flexible solutions, HR can mitigate disruptions and uphold employee well-being while maintaining organizational resilience.

Tactical Play:

- **Crisis Communication Plan:** Develop a comprehensive crisis communication plan to ensure transparent and timely communication during challenging times.
- **Team Training:** Train HR personnel to respond effectively to crises, understanding it as preparing players for unpredictable moves in a game.
- **Collaboration with Stakeholders:** Establish strong partnerships with key stakeholders, creating a network that supports effective crisis management.

Employee Well-being - The Defensive Line Against Burnout

As the defensive line protects against offensive scoring, HR's focus on employee well-being forms a defensive line against burnout and disengagement. By prioritizing initiatives that promote physical and mental health, your company can boost employee engagement, productivity, and retention while demonstrating a commitment to overall workforce welfare.

Tactical Play:

- **Well-being Programs:** Implement well-being initiatives to promote physical and mental health among employees.
- **Work-Life Balance:** Advocate for work-life balance policies to prevent burnout and enhance overall job satisfaction.
- **Employee Assistance Programs:** Provide resources and support systems for employees facing personal or professional challenges.

Succession Planning - Safeguarding Against Talent Gaps

A resilient defense plans for the unexpected, ensuring there are capable substitutes ready to step in. In football, it's often referred to as the "The Next Man Up" philosophy. In HR, this translates to a strong succession planning strategy. By proactively grooming talent and creating clear pathways for advancement, organizations can mitigate risks associated with key personnel changes and maintain operational effectiveness.

Tactical Play:

- **Identify Key Roles:** Identify critical positions within the organization and assess the potential impact of vacancies.
- **Talent Development:** Implement programs for grooming internal talent, preparing them for future leadership roles.
- **Cross-training:** Encourage cross-training to ensure that employees possess the necessary skills.

Employee Relations - Nurturing a Positive Workplace Culture

A positive team culture boosts morale, and HR's focus on employee relations fosters a unified work environment that withstands challenges. By promoting open communication, addressing concerns promptly, and facilitating conflict resolution, the HR team can enhance morale, productivity, and overall employee satisfaction.

Tactical Play:

- **Conflict Resolution Procedures:** Establish clear procedures for resolving workplace conflicts, ensuring a harmonious team dynamic.
- **Employee Feedback Channels:** Create channels for employees to provide feedback, enhancing communication and trust.

- **Recognition Programs:** Implement recognition programs to acknowledge and celebrate employees, boosting morale and job satisfaction.

As you prepare your defensive strategy, remember that challenges are not setbacks but opportunities for growth and improvement. Embracing challenges with resilience and a growth mindset fosters innovation, resilience, and continuous development, ultimately leading to greater success and game-day achievements.

Special Teams Excellence - Maximizing HR Impact through Strategic Collaboration

In HR, special teams represent collaboration, driving maximum impact for the organization. As the CHRO, envision yourself as the special teams coach, guiding members with plays to achieve success.

Bill Walsh, the Super Bowl-winning coach of the San Francisco 49ers said it well "The achievements of an organization are the results of the combined effort of each individual".

Just like a well-coordinated special teams unit on the field, your HR strategies will maximize impact, ensuring that each member contributes to the organization's overall success.

Pregame Strategy - Assembling Your Special Teams

Similar to a coach hand-selecting players for the special teams unit, HR must strategically assemble teams with diverse skills and expertise to address specific organizational needs. Carefully selecting team members who complement each other and share a common vision will foster collaboration, maximize efficiency, and drive sustainable success.

Tactical Play:

- **Skills Assessment:** Identify the unique skills and strengths of HR team members, assigning roles based on expertise.

- **Cross-functional collaboration:** Promote collaboration between different HR functions, fostering a culture of shared knowledge and expertise.

- **Project-Specific Teams:** Form special teams dedicated to specific projects or initiatives, ensuring a targeted approach.

Talent Acquisition - Scouting for All-Star Players

Football special teams units are most successful when they are comprised of the most athletic, agile, top-performing athletes. HR's talent acquisition strategy operates functionally like a football team's need to scout all-star players who bring unique talents to the organization.

Utilizing creativity and fresh perspectives in your recruitment strategy can be a game changer for attracting top talent in today's job market. By thinking outside the box and leveraging innovative approaches such as Instagram, TikTok, X, LinkedIn, employer branding, and interactive recruiting events, your company can differentiate itself and capture the attention of sought-after candidates. Using a fresh perspective and approach not only showcases your company's culture and values but also cultivates excitement and engagement among potential hires in the marketplace.

Tactical Play:

- **Strategic Recruiting:** Develop targeted recruitment strategies to attract individuals with specialized skills and experience.

- **Diversity and Inclusion:** Ensure diversity within special teams, fostering a mix of perspectives.

- **Onboarding Excellence:** Implement specialized onboarding programs to integrate new team members seamlessly.

Learning and Development - The Playbook Refinement Process

Special team players must continuously refine their approach to be successful in each game. HR's learning and development initiatives are essential for nurturing talent, fostering professional growth, and staying competitive. By investing in continuous learning opportunities, your company will ensure that employees acquire new skills and drive innovation, ensuring continuous improvement and success.

Tactical Play:

- **Skill Enhancement Programs:** Design programs that enhance the skills and capabilities of employees within special teams.
- **Continuous Feedback:** Establish feedback loops to gather insights from special teams, refining strategies based on their experiences.
- **Customized Training:** Tailor training programs to address the unique needs of each special team member, maximizing their effectiveness.

Employee Engagement - Energizing the Crowd

Special teams have the power to immediately energize the crowd with a punt or kick-off return. HR's focus on employee engagement similarly uplifts the entire organization by fostering a positive workplace culture and inspiring great productivity and overall engagement.

Tactical Play:

- **Recognition Initiatives:** Implement targeted recognition programs to acknowledge contributions.
- **Feedback Channels:** Create specific channels for team members to provide feedback, fostering a culture of open communication.
- **Team-Building Activities:** Organize team-building activities that strengthen bonds, promoting collaboration. (It is important to

leverage special tactics when dealing with geographically dispersed teams)

HR Technology - The Game-Changing Technology Play

HR's use of technology is its game-changing play, streamlining processes and enhancing overall efficiency. Emerging HR technologies include AI-enhanced employee self-service capabilities, automated recruiting and onboarding operations, reduced manual efforts, and time-intensive processes, ultimately enabling focus on strategic initiatives and enhancing overall operational efficiency.

Tactical Play:

- **Tech Stack Optimization:** Continuously assess and optimize the HR technology stack to ensure it aligns with evolving organizational needs. Additionally, stay abreast of emerging trends and offerings by key vendors in the marketplace.
- **Data-Driven Insights:** Leverage technology for data-driven insights, allowing the team to make informed decisions.
- **Innovation:** Establish a culture of innovation within HR, encouraging the use of new technologies to simplify and streamline manually intensive tasks/processes.

As you lead your HR team with a championship standard focus on Special Teams, envision each HR function as a specialized unit contributing its strengths to optimize the organizational playbook and contributing to your overall strategy.

The Hall of Fame Mindset - Elevating HR Leadership through Valuable Contributions

Adopting the Hall of Fame Mindset embodies a culture of

recognition and appreciation for the unique contributions of every team member, regardless of their role or position within the organization. It emphasizes the importance of acknowledging and valuing individual strengths, skills, and perspectives, recognizing that leveraging these diverse talents is instrumental in driving organizational success.

By fostering an inclusive environment where each member feels empowered to contribute their best, you can harness the collective power of the team to achieve shared goals and propel the organization forward.

Leadership Alignment - Uniting for a Common Goal

Just as a team will rally around a star player, HR's Hall of Fame Mindset involves aligning leadership around a common goal and recognizing each leader's unique strengths.

Tactical Play:

- **Leadership Assessments:** Conduct assessments to identify the unique strengths of HR leaders, aligning them with strategic organizational goals.
- **Collaborative Leadership:** Foster a collaborative leadership culture, ensuring each leader contributes their Hall of Fame qualities to the overall strategy.
- **Goal Setting:** Facilitate goal-setting sessions to align leadership with organizational objectives, creating a unified vision.

Employee Empowerment - Unleashing the Potential of Every Player

Just as a star player empowers teammates to perform at their best, the Hall of Fame Mindset involves empowering every employee to contribute their best, recognizing their strengths and achievements.

Tactical Play:

- **Skills Utilization:** Identify and leverage the unique skills of each employee, ensuring they contribute to areas where they excel.

- **Employee Development Plans:** Implement personalized development plans to improve individual strengths and enhance overall capabilities.

- **Recognition Programs:** Establish programs that celebrate and acknowledge employees for their contributions, fostering a culture of appreciation.

Strategic Partnerships - Building All-Star Collaborations

Star players often form alliances on the field for maximum impact. In HR, the Hall of Fame Mindset extends to building strategic partnerships across the company to foster overall success.

Tactical Play:

- **Cross-functional collaboration:** Encourage collaboration between HR and other departments, creating synergies for strategic initiatives.

- **External Partnerships:** Form alliances with external organizations, leveraging shared expertise and resources for mutual benefit.

- **Strategic Alliances:** Identify key stakeholders within the organization and build strategic alliances to support HR's initiatives.

Performance Metrics - Quantifying HR Impact

Just as a star player's performance is measured by statistics, HR's Hall of Fame Mindset involves quantifying the impact of HR strategies through KPIs. HR KPIs play a key role in assessing the effectiveness of HR strategies and initiatives, providing measurable insights into the impact of HR practices on organizational performance. Utilizing KPIs not only enhances accountability and transparency within the HR function but also demonstrates HR's value proposition in contributing to overall business objectives.

Tactical Play:

- **Establishing KPIs:** Define key performance indicators (KPIs) that align with organizational goals, providing measurable benchmarks for success.

- **Regular Performance Reviews:** Conduct regular reviews to assess the effectiveness of HR strategies and adjust approaches based on performance metrics.

- **Data-Driven Decision-Making:** Use data analytics to make informed, fact-based decisions, ensuring HR initiatives contribute meaningfully to organizational success.

Continuous Improvement - Striving for Perfection

Star players are known for their commitment to continuous improvement. Similarly, HR's Hall of Fame Mindset involves a pursuit of excellence and refinement.

Tactical Play:

- **Feedback Loops:** Establish feedback loops for HR processes, gathering insights for continuous improvement.

- **Professional Development:** Invest in ongoing professional development for HR professionals, ensuring they stay at the forefront of industry trends.

- **Innovation Initiatives:** Encourage a culture of innovation within HR, fostering a mindset of continuous improvement and adaptability.

As you instill the Hall of Fame Mindset within your HR team, envision every HR member as a valuable player contributing to the success of the entire organization. The upcoming chapters will highlight strategies to amplify the Hall of Fame Mindset, ensuring that HR's contributions are not only recognized but celebrated.

Building Your Championship Team

- ✓ Recruitment Blitz – Scoring Top Talent for Your Team
- ✓ Training Camp – Shaping Champions Through Comprehensive Development
- ✓ Team Cohesion Strategies – Forging Unity in the HR Huddle
- ✓ Leadership Development Drills – Creating Leaders on the HR Frontline
- ✓ Winning Culture – Cultivating Excellence in the HR Stadium

Recruitment Blitz - Scoring Top Talent for Your Team

The recruitment process is an important offensive drive with the end zone and a score representing the acquisition of top-tier talent. In HR, the Recruitment Blitz serves as your playbook, designed to secure the most skilled players for your team.

Bear Bryant, the University of Alabama football coach who coached his team to six national championships, once said, "It's not the will to win that matters—everyone has that. It's the will to prepare to win that matters."

By clearly defining recruitment goals, identifying target candidate profiles, and outlining recruitment strategies, your company can streamline hiring efforts and ensure alignment with business objectives. Additionally, establishing timelines, allocating resources effectively, and implementing measurement metrics enables your team to track progress, adapt to changing needs, and optimize the recruitment process for success. Through proactive planning and strategic execution, your company can enhance its ability to attract, engage, and retain the best-fit candidates, driving long-term organizational success.

This chapter provides tactics to help ensure your recruitment strategies are effective and leave an impact.

Blitz Preparation - Game Plan for Talent Acquisition

Just as a football team prepares a game plan to blitz the quarterback at key timeframes within the game, HR's Recruitment Blitz involves preparation to attract and secure the best talent.

Strategic Moves:

- **Talent Mapping:** Identify key positions and skills needed for organizational success, creating a talent map for targeted recruitment.
- **Competitor Analysis:** Analyze competitors to understand their talent pool, and compensation offerings, and create strategies to attract top performers.
- **Branding Initiatives:** Enhance the organization's employer brand through marketing campaigns and employee testimonials to attract top talent.

Playbook Development - Crafting Compelling Job Descriptions

A successful Recruitment Blitz requires a compelling playbook, and in HR, this translates to creating detailed job descriptions not only to help candidates understand the role and its requirements but also to enable recruiters to target their sourcing efforts effectively.

Strategic Moves:

- **Storytelling Elements:** Infuse storytelling elements into job descriptions, highlighting the organization's mission, values, and workplace culture.
- **Clear Expectations:** Clearly outline job responsibilities, expectations, and growth opportunities to set realistic expectations of the employee value proposition for potential candidates.
- **SEO & Job Board Optimization:** Optimize job descriptions for search engines and social media channels, with #keywords and #metadata to increase visibility and attract a broader range of candidates.

Team Collaboration - Coordinated Efforts for Maximum Impact

Just as a successful blitz involves coordinated efforts from every player, HR's Recruitment Blitz requires seamless collaboration between the hiring team, recruiters, and other stakeholders.

Strategic Moves:

- **Cross-Functional Teams:** Form cross-functional hiring teams with representatives from HR, department heads, and potential team members for inclusive perspectives.
- **Effective Communication:** Establish clear communication channels within the hiring team to ensure everyone is aligned with recruitment goals and strategies.
- **Training and Resources:** Provide training and necessary resources to hiring teams to enhance their recruitment skills and efficiency.

Talent Engagement - Building Relationships with Prospects

In a Recruitment Blitz, engagement is key. Engagement during the recruitment process is vital as it demonstrates respect for candidates' time and efforts while fostering a positive impression of the organization. Providing candidates with updates and feedback throughout the process not only maintains their interest but also instills confidence that their application is being considered seriously, ensuring a positive candidate experience, and enhancing the employer brand.

Strategic Moves:

- **Personalized Outreach:** Implement personalized outreach strategies, such as targeted emails, to connect with potential candidates on a personal level.
- **Virtual Events:** Host virtual events, webinars, or networking sessions to allow candidates to interact with current employees and gain insights into the organization.
- **Social Media Presence:** Leverage social media platforms to engage with potential candidates, sharing company culture, achievements, and employee stories.

Agile Adaptation - Adjusting Strategies Mid-Blitz

Just as a football team adjusts its strategies during a blitz, HR's Recruitment Blitz involves agile adaptation to market trends, candidate feedback, and evolving organizational needs.

Strategic Moves:

- **Continuous Feedback Loops:** Establish continuous feedback loops with hiring teams and candidates to adapt recruitment strategies based on real-time insights.

- **Market Trend Analysis:** Stay informed about market trends, competitor strategies, and industry changes to adjust recruitment approaches accordingly.

- **Flexibility in Offerings:** Be flexible in terms of compensation, benefits, and work arrangements to align with the preferences of top-tier candidates.

Performance Metrics - Scoring Recruitment Success

In a Recruitment Blitz, scoring is essential. Defining KPIs for the recruitment process is crucial for evaluating its effectiveness and identifying areas for improvement. By tracking metrics such as time-to-fill, quality of hires, and cost-per-hire, your team can make data-driven decisions, optimize recruitment strategies, and ensure alignment with business goals, ultimately driving greater efficiency and success with your talent acquisition initiatives.

Strategic Moves:

- **Time-to-Fill Metrics:** Track the time it takes to fill open positions, ensuring efficiency in the recruitment process.

- **Quality of Hire:** Assess the quality of hires based on performance, cultural fit, and long-term contributions to the organization.

- **Candidate Experience Surveys:** Gather feedback from candidates to evaluate their experience throughout the recruitment process and identify areas for improvement.

Training Camp - Shaping Champions through Comprehensive Development

Football teams hone their skills and build cohesion during training camp. HR's Training Camp is where employees forge their capabilities and team synergy.

Camp Preparation - Designing a Robust Training Curriculum

The success of any training camp lies in its curriculum. In HR, the Training Camp involves thorough planning to design a comprehensive program that addresses skill gaps, fosters growth, and aligns with organizational goals.

Strategic Moves:

- **Skills Assessment:** Conduct a thorough skills assessment to identify gaps and areas for improvement across the organization.
- **Goal Alignment:** Ensure that the training curriculum aligns with organizational goals, emphasizing skills that contribute to overall success.
- **Modular Structure:** Design the training program to be easily accessible and in modular form, allowing flexibility and customization based on the needs of employees.

Facilitators and Coaches - Nurturing Growth and Skill Mastery

Just as football players benefit from skilled coaches to show them improvement techniques, employees in HR's Training Camp need effective facilitators and mentors to guide them through the learning journey.

Strategic Moves:

- **Expert Facilitators:** Enlist subject matter experts or external trainers to provide in-depth knowledge and practical insights.

- **Internal Coaches:** Develop internal coaching programs, where experienced employees mentor and guide their peers in specific skill areas.

- **Continuous Feedback:** Facilitate regular feedback sessions to ensure that training is relevant, engaging, and meets the evolving needs of participants.

Immersive Learning - Simulating Real-World Scenarios

Training camp success lies in its ability to replicate real-world challenges. HR's Training Camp should immerse participants in lifelike scenarios, preparing the team for the complexities of their roles.

Strategic Moves:

- **Role-Playing Exercises:** Incorporate role-playing exercises that mimic common workplace scenarios, allowing participants to apply learned skills in a safe environment.

- **Case Studies:** Present real case studies that challenge participants to analyze, strategize, and make decisions as they would in their day-to-day roles.

- **Simulations:** Utilize technology to create realistic simulations that immerse participants in various aspects of HR, from conflict resolution to strategic planning.

Team Building - Fostering Collaboration and Cohesion

A cohesive team is essential for success, whether on the football field or in the workplace. HR's Training Camp should emphasize team-building activities that strengthen relationships and improve collaboration.

Strategic Moves:

- **Collaborative Projects:** Design training exercises that require collaboration, encouraging participants to work together toward common goals.

- **Team Challenges:** Introduce friendly competition, gamification, and challenges that promote teamwork among participants.

- **Cross-functional collaboration:** Facilitate interactions between employees from different departments to build cross-functional understanding and cooperation.

Continuous Development - Beyond the Initial Camp

Training Camp is not a one-time event; it's an ongoing process. HR professionals should establish mechanisms for continuous learning and development beyond the initial training period. By investing in employee training and skill development initiatives, your company can enhance workforce capabilities, adapt to evolving industry trends, and maintain a competitive edge in the market. Moreover, offering opportunities for continuous learning not only boosts employee engagement and satisfaction but also enables individuals to reach their full potential and drive organizational success.

Strategic Moves:

- **Online Learning Platforms:** Implement online learning platforms that offer a repository of resources, courses, and tools for continuous self-directed learning.
- **Mentorship Programs:** Establish mentorship programs that pair seasoned employees with newcomers, providing ongoing guidance and support.
- **Feedback Loops:** Create feedback mechanisms to gather insights on the effectiveness of training initiatives, allowing for continuous improvement.

Performance Metrics - Evaluating Training Effectiveness

Just as a coach continuously assesses player performance, HR must evaluate the effectiveness of its Training Camp. Defining key performance metrics ensures that the training program aligns with organizational goals.

KPIs for the effectiveness of training initiatives can include metrics such as training completion rates, post-training assessment scores, and on-the-job performance improvements. By tracking these indicators, your company can assess the impact of your training programs, identify areas for enhancement, and ensure that training investments align with strategic goals and objectives.

Strategic Moves:

- **Skill Mastery Assessments:** Conduct assessments to measure participants' mastery of key skills covered during the training.
- **Application Metrics:** Evaluate how well participants apply learned skills in their day-to-day roles, measuring the practical impact of the training.
- **Employee Satisfaction:** Collect feedback from participants to gauge overall satisfaction with the training experience and identify areas for improvement.

Envision your Training Camp as the breeding ground for champions. The following section provides insights into specific methodologies, approaches, and tools to ensure your Training Camp propels your team toward excellence.

Team Cohesion Strategies - Forging Unity in the HR Huddle

Football teams thrive on unity, and similarly, HR's strength lies in the seamless collaboration of its team members. team cohesion strategies are the playbook for creating a unified HR team ready to tackle any challenge.

Unity in Diversity - Embracing Differences for Strength

A high-performing team in HR recognizes and values diversity. Just as a strong football team is built with players with unique skills, backgrounds, and positions, the HR team plays a pivotal role in leading by example by leveraging diverse perspectives and expertise to foster an inclusive workplace culture that values innovation, collaboration, and mutual respect.

Strategic Moves:

- **Diversity Training:** Implement training programs that foster understanding and appreciation for diverse perspectives within the team.
- **Inclusive Culture:** Cultivate an inclusive culture where every team member feels valued, respected, and included.
- **Cross-functional collaboration:** Encourage collaboration between team members with different specialties to leverage a broad range of skills.

Clear Communication Channels - The Quarterback-Center Connection

In football, the quarterback and center must communicate successfully to execute the play and avoid the risk of mishandling the ball exchange. In HR, effective communication channels are vital for ensuring that information flows smoothly within the team.

Strategic Moves:

- **Regular Team Meetings:** Schedule regular team meetings to discuss ongoing projects, share updates, and address any challenges.
- **Transparent Communication:** Foster an environment of transparency, where team members feel comfortable sharing their thoughts, ideas, and concerns.
- **Utilize Collaboration Tools:** Implement modern collaboration tools to streamline communication, ensuring everyone is on the same page.

Shared Goals and Objectives - Working Towards the Endzone

Just as a football team works together to reach the endzone to score as many points as possible, the power of HR lies within team cohesion and is strengthened when everyone is aligned with a common vision, goals, and objectives.

Strategic Moves:

- **Goalsetting sessions:** Conduct collaborative goal-setting sessions to define short-term and long-term objectives for the HR team.

- **Individual Contribution to Team Goals:** Ensure that each team member understands their role in achieving shared goals, fostering a sense of collective responsibility.

- **Celebrate Achievements:** Acknowledge and celebrate milestones and successes, reinforcing the shared commitment to reaching organizational objectives.

Team Building Activities - Building Camaraderie Off the Field

Football teams engage in yearly team-building activities to ensure bonds are established and cultivated. Similarly, HR teams can also benefit from these types of activities that further define and build interpersonal relationships.

Strategic Moves:

- **Offsite Workshops:** Organize offsite training or workshops that provide team members with opportunities to bond in a relaxed setting.

- **Team-Building Exercises:** Incorporate team-building exercises into regular workdays to break routine and enhance collaboration. (Special tactics need to be considered to support those in geographically dispersed locations)

- **Social Events:** Plan social events, whether virtual or in-person, to create informal settings for team members to connect on a personal level. (Special tactics need to be considered to support those in geographically dispersed locations)

Conflict Resolution Strategies - Intercepting Challenges Before They Escalate

Intercepting a pass in football can change the momentum and overall course of the game. Similarly, intercepting and resolving conflicts effectively is crucial for maintaining a harmonious work environment and preventing larger issues from escalating.

Through proactive conflict management strategies, HR can address interpersonal disputes promptly, foster open communication, and implement mediation techniques to facilitate resolution, ultimately promoting a positive and productive workplace culture.

Strategic Moves:

- **Mediation Training:** Provide training on conflict resolution and mediation techniques to HR team members.
- **Establishing Clear Protocols:** Define clear protocols for addressing conflicts, ensuring that issues are resolved promptly and fairly.
- **Encourage Open Dialogue:** Create an environment where team members feel comfortable expressing concerns and discussing conflicts openly.

Recognition and Appreciation - Touchdown Celebrations for Team Achievements

By now, we have all seen unique touchdown celebrations during a football game. By acknowledging and celebrating your teams' contributions and achievements, you can boost morale, enhance job satisfaction, and increase employee engagement, ultimately leading to improved performance and retention.

Strategic Moves:

- **Regular Recognition Programs:** Institute regular recognition programs that highlight exceptional contributions by team members.
- **Peer Recognition:** Encourage team members to recognize and appreciate each other's efforts, fostering a positive and collaborative atmosphere.

- **Celebratory Rituals:** Establish celebratory rituals for team achievements, creating a sense of shared accomplishment.

The following section highlights techniques to execute these strategies effectively, ensuring that your team operates with precision and unity.

Leadership Development Drills – Creating Leaders on the HR Frontline

In football, leadership is honed through drills that simulate game scenarios. Similarly, leadership development drills are the training ground for cultivating effective HR leaders who can navigate the organizational playing field.

Identifying Leadership Potential - Scouting the HR Talent Pool

Just as football coach scouts for talented players, HR leaders need to identify potential leaders within their team. Leadership development drills begin with recognizing the talent that can be molded into future HR leaders.

Strategic Moves:

- **Assessment Tools:** Utilize leadership assessment tools and 360 peer feedback reviews to identify individuals with the potential for leadership roles.
- **Performance Reviews:** Regularly assess team members' performance and potential for leadership responsibilities.
- **Feedback Mechanisms:** Establish feedback mechanisms to gather insights from peers and supervisors on leadership potential.

Mentorship Programs - Coaching for HR Success

In football, veteran players often mentor younger players. HR leadership development drills involve establishing mentorship programs that provide guidance and coaching for up-and-coming HR leaders.

Strategic Moves:

- **Pairing Mentors and Mentees:** Match experienced HR leaders with emerging talents to create mentorship pairs.
- **Structured Mentorship Sessions:** Develop a structured program with regular mentorship sessions covering leadership principles, challenges, and opportunities.
- **Goal-Setting Discussions:** Encourage mentors to guide mentees in setting and achieving leadership development goals.

Simulated Leadership Challenges - The HR Scrimmage

Just as a football team scrimmages to simulate game day conditions, HR leadership development drills involve simulated challenges to prepare emerging leaders for real-world scenarios.

Strategic Moves:

- **Case Studies and Role-Playing:** Develop case studies and role-playing scenarios that mimic HR leadership challenges.
- **Team Collaboration Exercises:** Design exercises that require leaders to collaborate with team members to solve complex HR issues.
- **Feedback and Debriefing:** After each simulated challenge, conduct thorough feedback sessions to identify strengths and areas for improvement.

Continuous Learning Initiatives - The HR Training Camp

In football, players attend training camps to enhance their skills. HR leaders, too, must engage in continuous learning initiatives to stay abreast of industry trends and evolving leadership practices.

Strategic Moves:

- **Leadership Workshops and Seminars:** Organize workshops and seminars focused on leadership development topics.
- **Encourage the Pursuit of Advanced Degrees:** Support and incentivize HR leaders to pursue advanced degrees or certifications in leadership.
- **HR associations and Knowledge Sharing:** Establish forums for leaders to engage in knowledge-sharing sessions, fostering a culture of continuous learning.

Team Leadership Exercises - Cohesive Leadership at Play

Just as a football team practices coordinated plays, HR leaders must engage in exercises that promote cohesive leadership within the team.

Strategic Moves:

- **Cross-Functional Team Projects:** Assign HR leaders to cross-functional projects that require collaborative leadership.
- **Team-Building Workshops:** Organize workshops focused on team building and leadership development.
- **360-Degree Feedback:** Implement 360-degree feedback mechanisms to gather insights on leadership effectiveness from peers, subordinates, and superiors.

Succession Planning - Building a Bench of HR Leaders

In football, teams plan for the future by drafting a strong bench of players. Similarly, HR leadership development drills include succession planning to ensure a pipeline of capable leaders.

Strategic Moves:

- **Identify Key Roles:** Identify critical HR roles and potential future leadership positions.

- **Individual Development Plans:** Work with emerging leaders to create individual development plans tailored to their leadership aspirations.
- **Regular Succession Reviews:** Conduct regular reviews of succession plans to adapt to changing organizational needs.

The next section provides techniques to execute these drills effectively, ensuring that your team is not only prepared for the game but is ready to lead with confidence and agility.

Winning Culture - Cultivating Excellence in the HR Stadium

In football, a winning culture is the heartbeat of a successful team. Similarly, in the HR stadium, cultivating a winning culture is the key to unlocking the full potential of your team and driving success on all fronts.

Defining Winning Culture in HR - The Blueprint for Success

The playbook is the most important tool for a football team. Similarly, a strong technique to implement as the CHRO is to establish a playbook for defining and instilling a winning culture. A dedicated HR handbook plays a crucial role in instilling cultural norms within the HR department, serving as a guide for internal practices and behaviors that reflect the organization's values. By outlining HR-specific policies, procedures, and ethical standards, the handbook ensures consistency and alignment with the broader organizational culture.

Strategic Moves:

- **Core Values Definition:** Clearly articulate the core values that define the desired culture within the HR team.
- **Cultural Alignment:** Align HR practices and processes with the defined core values to ensure consistency.

- **Leadership Exemplification:** Leaders must embody the desired culture through their actions, setting the tone for the entire team.

Fostering a Positive Work Environment - The Locker Room Spirit

In football, the locker room is a safe space where team camaraderie is built. Similarly, HR leaders must create a positive work environment that fosters collaboration, trust, and a shared commitment to excellence.

Strategic Moves:

- **Open Communication Channels:** Establish open lines of communication to encourage transparency and feedback.
- **Recognition Programs:** Implement programs that recognize and celebrate individual and team achievements.
- **Team-Building Activities:** Organize regular team-building activities to strengthen bonds and foster a sense of belonging. (Special tactics must be employed to support geographically dispersed personnel)

Promoting Inclusivity and Diversity - The Strength of a Diverse Lineup

Football teams thrive on diversity, leveraging the unique strengths of each player. In HR, a Winning Culture embraces inclusivity and diversity as core pillars for success.

Strategic Moves:

- **Diversity Training:** Provide training on diversity and inclusion to enhance awareness and understanding.
- **Diverse Recruitment Practices:** Implement strategies to attract a diverse talent pool and ensure fair hiring practices.
- **Inclusive Policies:** Develop policies that promote an inclusive workplace, accommodating diverse perspectives and backgrounds.

Continuous Improvement Mindset - The Halftime Adjustment

The halftime period during a football game is an important timeframe to make adjustments and improvements for the second half of the game. Similarly, the HR team needs to adopt a continuous improvement mindset to adapt to evolving business needs and enhance HR practices. By seeking feedback, identifying areas for enhancement, and implementing iterative changes, the HR team can drive innovation, optimize processes, and better support organizational growth and success.

Strategic Moves:

- **Feedback Mechanisms:** Make feedback a common occurrence and establish regular feedback loops for employees to share insights on processes and work dynamics.
- **Continuous Learning Initiatives:** Encourage a culture of continuous learning and professional development.
- **Agile Approach:** Embrace an agile mindset, allowing the team to adapt to changing circumstances and seize opportunities for improvement.

Employee Well-being Initiatives - Peak Performance Conditioning

Football teams invest in the well-being of their players for peak performance. HR leaders must also prioritize employee well-being initiatives. Prioritizing these initiatives is paramount for creating a supportive and thriving workplace environment.

By investing in programs that promote physical health, mental wellness, and work-life balance, the HR team can lead by example in its commitment to nurturing employee happiness and productivity.

Moreover, fostering a culture of well-being not only enhances employee morale and engagement but also contributes to reduced absenteeism, higher retention rates, and overall organizational success.

Strategic Moves:

- **Mental Health Programs:** Implement programs that address mental health and stress management.
- **Work-Life Balance:** Promote policies and practices that support a healthy work-life balance.
- **Wellness Programs:** Introduce wellness initiatives that cater to the physical and mental well-being of employees.

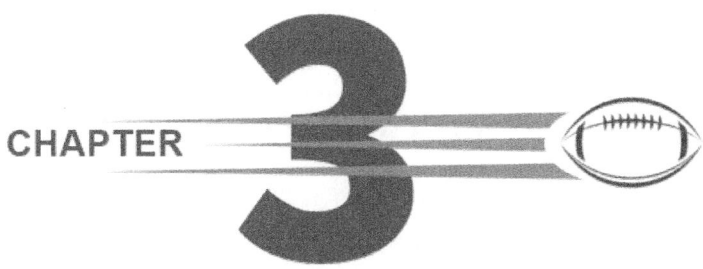

Scouting the Competition

✓ Market Research – Scouting the HR Landscape
✓ Competitor Analysis – Decoding the Opponents' Playbook
✓ Game Film Review – Strategic Insights from HR's Past Performance
✓ SWOT Analysis – Scouting Your HR Field
✓ Tactical Adjustments – Navigating the Dynamic HR Game

Market Research - Scouting the HR Landscape

As the CHRO, scouting the HR landscape can be difficult without insights based on data. Football coaches assess the strengths and weaknesses of their opponents through game tape, statistics, and other means.

You'll need to navigate the HR landscape, making informed decisions that position your organization for success in the game of talent management.

The Game Plan for HR Market Research

Football teams strategize based on their understanding of opponents; HR leaders must craft a game plan informed by comprehensive market research. Creating this plan involves identifying key objectives, defining target demographics, and selecting appropriate methodologies to gather relevant data.

By analyzing market trends, competitor practices, and talent demands, your team can gain valuable insights to inform strategic decision-making and enhance recruitment and retention strategies.

This section highlights key components of an effective HR market research game plan.

Strategic Moves:

- **Industry Benchmarking:** Conduct a thorough analysis of industry benchmarks to understand how your organization compares to competitors in terms of HR practices, compensation, and talent management.
- **Talent Availability Assessment:** Assess the current talent landscape, identifying the availability of skilled professionals and potential skill gaps.
- **Competitor Analysis:** Study the HR practices of competitors to identify best practices, potential gaps, and areas for differentiation.

The Talent Scouting Process - Identifying Key Players

Talent scouting, in football, is critical for building a team that can go undefeated during the season. Likewise, HR leaders must focus on identifying key players in the talent pool who align with the organization's goals and values.

Strategic Moves:

- **Skillset Identification:** Clearly define the skills and competencies required for success within the organization.
- **Pipeline Development:** Create a talent pipeline by proactively identifying and engaging with potential candidates.
- **Succession Planning:** Implement succession planning strategies to ensure a steady flow of talent for key roles within the organization.

Adapting to Market Trends - Agile Play calling

Offensive coordinators consistently adjust their play calling based on the game's progress. Similarly, HR leaders must adopt an agile approach to play calling by staying attuned to evolving market trends.

Strategic Moves:

- **Continuous Monitoring:** Establish mechanisms for continuous monitoring of HR and talent management trends.
- **Technology Integration:** Embrace emerging HR technologies that can enhance recruitment processes and talent management.
- **Feedback Loops:** Incorporate feedback from current employees, candidates, recruiters, and industry experts to refine HR strategies.

Diversity and Inclusion Insights - A Diverse Lineup for Victory

In HR, understanding diversity and inclusion trends is important to building a winning team.

Strategic Moves:

- **D&I Metrics Analysis:** Analyze diversity and inclusion metrics to identify areas of improvement and success.

- **Inclusive Recruitment Practices:** Implement recruitment strategies that foster diversity, ensuring fair and equitable hiring practices.

- **Cultural Sensitivity Training:** Provide training to HR teams on cultural sensitivity to create an inclusive workplace.

The Competitive Advantage - Leveraging Market Insights

HR leaders can turn market insights into a competitive advantage. By crafting talent strategies that utilize market insights, addressing industry challenges, and capitalizing on emerging opportunities, your team can tailor recruitment, development, and retention initiatives to meet evolving business needs.

Strategic Moves:

- **Customized Talent Strategies:** Develop tailored talent strategies based on market insights and organizational goals.

- **Predictive Analytics:** Explore the use of predictive analytics to anticipate future talent needs and challenges.

- **Strategic Partnerships:** Build strategic partnerships with educational institutions, industry associations, and other entities to access top talent.

The following section provides tips for each strategic move, offering steps to conduct effective market research and position your HR team as a strategic player in the talent game.

Competitor Analysis - Decoding the Opponent's Playbook

In football, understanding your opponent's strengths and weaknesses is the key to victory. Similarly, in HR, a thorough competitor analysis is your playbook for deciphering industry rivals and crafting strategies that outshine the competition. In some cases, the HR team can leverage Glassdoor.com as a valuable resource to gain insights into competitors' employee experiences, company cultures, and recruitment practices. By analyzing reviews, ratings, and feedback from current and former employees, the HR team can identify trends, strengths, weaknesses, and areas for improvement within competitor organizations.

Scouting the HR Field - Understanding Competitors

Just as football teams study the strategies of upcoming opponents, researching the practices of your competitors can provide valuable insights into your potential adjustments for the season.

Strategic Moves:

- **Identifying Key Competitors:** Identify main competitors in the industry and those vying for top talent in your sector.
- **Organizational Structure:** Analyze the organizational structure of competitors to understand how they manage their HR functions.
- **HR Policies and Practices:** Dive into the specifics of competitors' HR policies, from recruitment and training to talent management, compensation, and employee engagement. Again, Glassdoor.com is a solid resource for baseline information.

Talent Game Tapes - Analyzing Competitors' Playbooks

Football teams routinely analyze game tapes to anticipate opponents' strategies and plays. Likewise, HR leaders should regularly scrutinize competitors' playbooks, or talent strategies, to discern successful tactics and areas for enhancement. This proactive approach allows HR to stay ahead in the game of talent acquisition and management.

Strategic Moves:

- **Recruitment Strategies:** Examine competitors' approaches to attracting and retaining talent, including their recruitment channels, employer branding, and employee value propositions.

- **Training and Development:** Evaluate competitors' investments in employee training and development to glean insights into skill enhancement and career progression.

- **Employee Engagement Initiatives:** Study competitors' initiatives for employee engagement, recognizing successful practices that contribute to a positive workplace culture.

HR Technology Stack - Uncovering Technological Advancements

Just as football teams invest in cutting-edge technology for personnel training and game-time decision enhancement, HR leaders should also explore competitors' HR technology stacks. This analysis unveils the tools and platforms that give competitors a technological advantage in managing their workforce. Some of this information can be obtained through various sources, including industry reports, surveys conducted by HR associations, and professional networking groups.

Strategic Moves:

- **HRIS Systems:** Investigate the Human Resources Information Systems (HRIS) used by competitors, focusing on functionalities and user experiences.

- **Performance Management Tools:** Explore tools for performance management and feedback to understand how competitors measure employee performance.

- **Data Analytics Capabilities:** Assess competitors' data analytics capabilities in HR, identifying areas where technology is leveraged for strategic decision-making.

Compensation and Benefits Benchmarking - Winning the Talent War

The role of a football team's general manager extends beyond mere player recruitment; it involves the delicate balance of managing the salary cap while striving to attract top talent. Understanding competitors' compensation and benefits structures is paramount for HR leaders to ensure their organization remains competitive in the talent market. Just as a general manager meticulously assesses the market value of star players, HR professionals must conduct thorough research to offer attractive compensation packages.

Moreover, they must tailor these packages to not only attract but also retain key employees in a competitive landscape. By adopting a strategic approach akin to a general manager's salary cap management, HR leaders can effectively allocate resources to secure top talent while staying within budgetary constraints.

Strategic Moves:

- **Salary Structures:** Compare competitors' salary structures to gauge how your organization aligns with industry standards.
- **Benefits Packages:** Evaluate the range and appeal of benefits offered by competitors, including healthcare, retirement plans, and additional perks.
- **Employee Recognition Programs:** Investigate how competitors acknowledge and reward employee contributions, providing insights into effective recognition strategies.

Success Metrics - Scoring Insights from Competitors

In football, success is not solely determined by the final scoreboard but can also be assessed through various performance metrics, such as the speed at which the quarterback releases the football during a pass or the efficiency of defensive tackles in stopping the opposing team's offense. Similarly, HR leaders gauge success not only by the number of new hires but also by their ability to attract and retain top talent in a competitive market. By leveraging metrics such as time-to-fill, turnover rates, and employee satisfaction scores, HR can gain insights into their organization's competitive position and make data-driven decisions to adjust their strategies for ongoing success.

Strategic Moves:

- **Retention Rates:** Analyze competitors' retention rates to understand the effectiveness of their talent retention strategies.
- **Employee Satisfaction Surveys:** Investigate the use of employee satisfaction surveys by competitors, identifying areas of strength and improvement.
- **Time-to-Fill Metrics:** Evaluate the time it takes for competitors to fill key positions, providing insights into their recruitment efficiency.

Competitive Edge - Crafting Your Winning Play

In HR, conducting a competitor analysis is like studying game tapes before a championship game. By carefully evaluating the data collected from competitors' talent strategies, compensation packages, and employee benefits offerings, HR professionals can gain valuable insights into industry trends and best practices.

Armed with this knowledge, they can make strategic moves to strengthen their company's position in the market, whether it's by refining their recruitment strategies, optimizing compensation plans, or enhancing employee engagement initiatives. Just as a football coach studies game tapes to identify the opposing team's strengths and weaknesses, HR leaders use competitor analysis to inform their decision-making process and stay ahead of the competition.

Game Film Review - Strategic Insights from HR's Past Performance

To improve, it is essential to review past performance. Game Film Review in HR provides valuable insights, allowing you to capitalize on tactics that worked well, to ensure you don't repeat mistakes, and to elevate your team's overall effectiveness.

Reflecting on Past Plays - The Importance of Self-Analysis

Before strategizing for future games, football teams perform a thorough review of their past performances. Similarly, in HR, analyzing past plays – your organization's HR practices – is vital for continuous improvement.

Strategic Moves:

- **Audit of HR Processes:** Conduct a comprehensive audit of your HR processes, including recruitment, onboarding, performance management, benefits, and talent development.
- **Effectiveness Evaluation:** Assess the effectiveness of past HR initiatives, compliance, and programs, identifying successful strategies and areas requiring enhancement.
- **Feedback and Surveys:** Utilize employee feedback and surveys to gauge satisfaction with HR practices, ensuring a comprehensive understanding of the employee experience.

Identifying Wins and Losses - Celebrate Success, Learn from Setbacks

Identifying wins and losses and learning from past performance involves objectively evaluating successes and shortcomings to identify areas for improvement and optimization.

By conducting thorough assessments of past initiatives, projects, and outcomes, your team can pinpoint specific areas where performance fell short of expectations or where opportunities for enhancement exist. This process enables teams to extract valuable lessons, implement corrective actions, and refine strategies to achieve a roadmap for shaping future strategies.

Strategic Moves:

- **Recognition of Success:** Celebrate HR successes, acknowledging initiatives that positively impact employee engagement, talent retention, or organizational culture.

- **Learning from Challenges:** Analyze setbacks or challenges faced with existing HR processes, explore root causes, and formulate strategies to overcome similar obstacles in the future.

- **Employee Feedback Integration:** Incorporate employee feedback into the review process, ensuring insights from the workforce contribute to the evaluation of HR performance.

Key Performance Indicators (KPIs) - Metrics for HR Success

Football teams track key metrics, such as first-down percentages, passing completions, rushing yards, touchdowns, and turnovers. Similarly, HR leaders must identify and measure Key Performance Indicators (KPIs) to assess the success of their initiatives.

Strategic Moves:

- **Define HR KPIs:** Clearly define KPIs aligned with HR goals, such as employee satisfaction, talent retention rates, and the effectiveness of training programs.

- **Data Analytics Utilization:** Leverage data analytics tools to gather and analyze HR performance data, providing a quantitative basis for decision-making.

- **Continuous Monitoring:** Establish a system for continuous monitoring of HR KPIs, allowing for real-time adjustments and improvements.

Employee Development Plays - Building a Winning Roster

Focusing on employee development efforts is essential for nurturing a skilled and engaged workforce capable of driving organizational success. By investing in training, mentorship programs, and career development initiatives, organizations empower employees to enhance their skills, expand their knowledge, and realize their full potential.

Moreover, fostering a culture of continuous learning and growth not only improves employee satisfaction and retention but also strengthens the organization's competitive advantage in the marketplace. Through strategic alignment of development efforts with business objectives, HR can ensure that employees are equipped with the skills and capabilities needed to adapt to evolving challenges and contribute to the company's long-term growth and prosperity.

Strategic Moves:

- **Training Program Evaluation:** Evaluate the effectiveness of past training programs in enhancing employee skills and competencies.
- **Career Development Initiatives:** Assess the impact of career development initiatives on employee satisfaction and retention.
- **Succession Planning:** Review the success of succession planning efforts, ensuring a pipeline of skilled talent for key positions.

Cultural Assessment - Defining Your Organizational Identity

Football teams have a distinct culture that defines their identity. Likewise, HR leaders must assess and shape the organizational culture to align with strategic objectives.

Strategic Moves:

- **Employee Surveys on Organizational Culture:** Administer surveys to gauge employee perceptions of the organizational culture, identifying strengths and areas for improvement.
- **Alignment with Values:** Assess the alignment of organizational values with actual practices, ensuring consistency in cultural messaging.
- **Leadership Role in Culture:** Evaluate the role of leadership in shaping and reinforcing the desired organizational culture.

Lessons from Defeats - Turning Setbacks into Opportunities

Even championship teams face defeats, but it's their ability to learn and rebound that defines their greatness. Similarly, in HR, turning setbacks into opportunities is a crucial aspect of continuous improvement.

Strategic Moves:

- **Root Cause Analysis:** Conduct a thorough root cause analysis of any HR-related setbacks, identifying systemic issues or external factors.
- **Adaptive Strategies:** Formulate adaptive strategies based on lessons learned from setbacks, ensuring preparedness for future challenges.
- **Communication and Transparency:** Communicate openly about setbacks and the corrective actions taken, fostering transparency and trust within the organization.

As you perform a game film review, envision your HR team dissecting every play to refine your playbook. The insights gained will shape the strategies outlined in the next section, guiding you toward HR excellence through reflective and forward-thinking practices.

SWOT Analysis - Scouting Your HR Field

Head football coaches, offensive, defense, and special team coordinators consistently evaluate their teams' strengths, weaknesses, opportunities, and threats (SWOT) on the field. In HR, conducting a SWOT analysis allows your team to gain valuable insights into internal strengths and weaknesses, as well as external opportunities and threats. By clarifying these findings, you and your team will be positioned to make informed decisions to adjust plans accordingly for the future.

Strengths - Capitalizing on Your HR Assets

In football, a team's strengths lie in its skilled players and strategic plays. Similarly, HR must identify and capitalize on its strengths to enhance organizational success.

Strategic Moves:

- **Talent Pool Assessment:** Evaluate the skills and expertise of your HR team, emphasizing areas of specialization and proficiency.
- **Technology and Tools:** Assess the effectiveness of HR technology and tools, leveraging advanced solutions to streamline processes.
- **Positive Culture:** Identify and amplify aspects of the organizational culture that contribute to a positive and productive workplace.

Weaknesses - Tackling HR Challenges Head-On

Football teams consistently work to overcome weaknesses and improve for the next game. Addressing HR challenges and weaknesses head-on is crucial for fostering continuous improvement and enhancing future performance.

By acknowledging and confronting these issues directly, you and your team can identify root causes, implement corrective actions, and develop proactive solutions to prevent recurrence. This proactive approach not only strengthens HR processes and practices but also fosters a culture of accountability, transparency, and resilience within the organization.

Strategic Moves:

- **Skill Gap Analysis:** Conduct a thorough analysis of skill gaps within the HR team, developing targeted training programs to address weaknesses.
- **Process Inefficiencies:** Identify inefficiencies in HR processes and workflows, implementing improvements to enhance efficiency.
- **Communication Challenges:** Address any communication challenges within the HR team, fostering open and transparent channels for collaboration.

Opportunities - Making Strategic Gains in HR

Football teams are built and trained to capitalize on impromptu opportunities during the game, and similarly, you and your team must also identify and seize opportunities for continuous improvement.

Strategic Moves:

- **Market Trends Exploration:** Explore current market trends in HR, identifying opportunities to adopt innovative practices or technologies.
- **Talent Acquisition:** Assess opportunities for talent acquisition, considering diverse talent pools and international markets.
- **Strategic Partnerships:** Explore potential partnerships with external organizations, vendors, or educational institutions to enhance HR capabilities.

Threats - Defending Against HR Risks

Defending against HR risks requires a proactive and comprehensive approach to identify, assess, and mitigate potential threats to the company. By conducting regular risk assessments and audits, you and your team can identify vulnerabilities in areas such as compliance, data security, and employee relations. Your company's position will be much stronger by proactively reviewing, enhancing, and implementing robust policies, procedures, and controls, along with providing ongoing training and education to support these potential issues.

Strategic Moves:

- **Legal and Compliance Risks:** Stay vigilant about changes in employment labor laws and compliance requirements, proactively addressing any potential risks.
- **Economic Downturn Preparedness:** Develop contingency plans for economic downturns or market uncertainties, ensuring HR strategies remain resilient.
- **Technological Disruptions:** Anticipate potential technological disruptions in HR practices, staying ahead of advancements to maintain competitiveness.

Integrating SWOT Findings - Shaping Your HR Game Plan

Leveraging SWOT findings empowers you and your HR team to develop a strategic game plan that capitalizes on strengths, addresses weaknesses, seizes opportunities, and mitigates threats.

By analyzing internal capabilities and external factors, you can identify areas for improvement, innovation, and growth within the organization. This approach enables you to align HR initiatives with overarching business objectives, ensuring a strong foundation for future success.

Strategic Moves:

- **Strategic Priority Alignment:** Align HR strategies with organizational priorities, ensuring that strengths and opportunities are maximized.
- **Mitigation of Weaknesses and Threats:** Develop targeted plans to mitigate weaknesses and address potential threats, minimizing their impact.

- **Agile Strategy Development:** Embrace an agile approach to strategy development, allowing for adaptability based on evolving strengths, weaknesses, opportunities, and threats.

Just as football teams scout their opponents, the SWOT analysis is your scouting report for the HR field. It positions you to play to your strengths, shore up weaknesses, seize opportunities, and tackle potential threats as you navigate the game of Human Resources.

Tactical Adjustments - Navigating the Dynamic HR Game

Successful football teams make real-time game adjustments to stay ahead of their opponents. Similarly, mastering the art of tactical adjustments and remaining agile is essential for fostering a continuous improvement culture within the HR team. In today's business environment, adaptability and responsiveness are paramount to effectively address evolving challenges and seize emerging opportunities. By embracing a mindset of continuous improvement, you and your HR team can proactively identify areas for optimization, refine strategies, and enhance processes to stay ahead of the curve.

Continuous Improvement Mindset

The continuous improvement mindset is crucial for driving organizational growth and HR success by fostering innovation and adaptability. Embracing this mindset encourages your team to constantly seek ways to enhance processes, products, and services, leading to increased efficiency and effectiveness.

Strategic Moves:

- **Feedback Mechanisms:** Establish feedback loops to gather insights from HR team members, employees, and key stakeholders.

- **Process Optimization:** Regularly review HR processes and identify areas for optimization, ensuring efficiency and effectiveness.

- **Learning and Development:** Invest in ongoing learning and development programs for HR professionals to stay abreast of industry best practices.

Agile Response to Market Shifts

Football coaches are masters at adapting strategies based on how the game unfolds. Similarly, responding with agility to shifts in the market and industry trends enables you and the HR team to stay ahead of the curve and capitalize on emerging opportunities. By closely monitoring market dynamics and promptly adjusting HR strategies and initiatives, you can effectively address changes to demands and organizational needs.

Strategic Moves:

- **Market Trend Monitoring:** Stay vigilant about emerging trends in HR, adapting strategies to capitalize on new opportunities.

- **Competitor Benchmarking:** Continuously benchmark HR practices against industry competitors, adopting innovations that enhance competitiveness.

- **Flexibility in Policies:** Design HR policies with flexibility to accommodate evolving market dynamics, ensuring relevance and alignment.

Employee Feedback Integration

Just as football coaches value player feedback, integrating employee feedback is essential for refining HR strategies and initiatives to better meet the needs and expectations of the workforce. By actively listening to employees' perspectives, concerns, and suggestions, you and your HR team can gain valuable insights into areas for improvement and innovation.

Strategic Moves:

- **Employee Surveys:** Regularly conduct surveys to gather feedback on HR programs, policies, and overall employee experience.

- **Focus Groups:** Establish focus groups to further analyze HR areas, using employee insights to inform decision-making.

- **Open Communication Channels:** Foster open communication channels for employees to provide real-time feedback, creating a responsive HR environment.

Technology Optimization

Football teams leverage technology for performance analysis, and optimizing the use of HR technology is paramount for your HR team to support streamlined operations and enhance efficiency. By leveraging advanced HR software and tools, you can automate routine tasks, streamline processes, and minimize manual efforts, allowing your team to focus on strategic initiatives and value-added activities.

Strategic Moves:

- **HR Technology Audits:** Conduct regular audits of HR technology systems, ensuring they align with organizational needs, compliance, and industry standards.

- **Integration Solutions:** Explore integration solutions for HR systems, enhancing a unified database, data flow, and eliminating silos.

- **Data-Driven Decision-Making:** Promote a data-driven HR culture, using analytics to make informed decisions and drive strategic initiatives.

Crisis Management Protocols

Having crisis management protocols in place is essential for effectively navigating unforeseen HR issues and mitigating potential risks to the company. By establishing clear procedures and communication channels, you can ensure swift and coordinated responses to crises, minimizing disruption and protecting the well-being of employees and the company's reputation. Additionally, proactive planning enables your HR team to anticipate potential scenarios, assess vulnerabilities, and develop contingency plans to address various contingencies.

Strategic Moves:

- **Scenario Planning:** Conduct scenario planning exercises to anticipate potential HR crises and develop response strategies.
- **Crisis Communication Plans:** Establish clear communication plans for HR crises, ensuring transparency and maintaining trust.
- **Agile Decision-Making:** Train HR teams in agile decision-making to respond swiftly and effectively to crises.

Effective HR leadership demands a playbook of tactical adjustments. By embracing a mindset of continuous improvement, responding to market shifts, integrating employee feedback, optimizing technology, and preparing for crises, you'll navigate the game of HR with resilience and success.

CHAPTER 4

Game Day Execution

✓ Pregame Rituals – Setting the HR Stage for Success
✓ Play Calling Strategies – Orchestrating Success
✓ Real-time Adaptation: Agility in HR Leadership
✓ Halftime Adjustments: Pivoting for HR Success
✓ Post-game Analysis: Extracting Insights for Future Wins

Pregame Rituals: Setting the HR Stage for Success

In HR leadership, success is an ongoing performance, crafted through intentional techniques. As the CHRO, envision the significance of pregame techniques as the foundation for improved performance.

To quote Vince Lombardi again, winner of five NFL championships in seven years, including two Super Bowls, once said, "The only place success comes before work is in the dictionary."

Techniques that Foster Team Unity

Just as football teams build camaraderie through pregame rituals, designing activities that unite the HR team and foster a sense of collective purpose is crucial for building strong bonds and enhancing collaboration.

By creating opportunities for team members to engage in shared experiences and common goals, you can strengthen relationships, boost morale, and cultivate a cohesive work environment.

Strategic Moves:

- **Team-Building Exercises:** Engage in team-building activities that promote collaboration, trust, and a shared commitment to HR goals.
- **Group Discussions:** Facilitate open discussions to encourage team members to share insights, challenges, and ideas, fostering a sense of belonging.
- **Vision and Mission Alignment:** Reiterate the HR department's vision and mission, reinforcing a collective understanding of its purpose.

Aligning HR Strategies with Organizational Goals

Football teams align their plays with overarching strategies and ensuring that HR strategies seamlessly align with the broader organizational goals is paramount for driving sustainable success and maximizing impact.

By closely aligning HR initiatives with the company's overarching objectives, you can ensure that talent management efforts directly contribute to strategic priorities and business outcomes.

This alignment enables HR to effectively support the organization's growth, innovation, and competitive advantage by cultivating a high-performing workforce aligned with the company's mission and values.

Strategic Moves:

- **Leadership Alignment:** First, ensure that you are aligned with the executive team, fostering a unified approach to organizational success.
- **Strategic Planning Sessions:** Conduct pregame planning sessions to align HR strategies with current organizational objectives.
- **Objective Setting:** Define clear HR objectives that contribute directly to the achievement of broader business goals.

Mental Preparation for HR Challenges

Just as athletes often have pre-game rituals that help them mentally prepare for the game, you should equip your team with a similar mindset needed to tackle HR challenges.

Strategic Moves:

- **Scenario Role-Playing:** Engage in scenario role-playing exercises to simulate potential HR challenges, preparing the team for effective responses.

- **Professional Development:** Provide ongoing training to enhance the skills and competencies of HR professionals, ensuring they are well-prepared for evolving challenges.
- **Mindfulness Practices:** Introduce mindfulness practices to help HR professionals manage stress and maintain focus in high-pressure situations.

Reviewing Employee Handbooks

The playbook of a football team is the most reviewed and coveted artifact of the team. In HR, the employee handbook serves as the foundational document for the company, outlining policies, procedures, and expectations to guide employees in their roles.

It provides clarity on company culture, values, and standards of conduct, fostering consistency and alignment across the workforce. Moreover, frequent reviews and updates of the handbook are essential to ensure it remains relevant and compliant with evolving laws, regulations, and industry standards.

By regularly revisiting and refining the handbook, your company can address emerging issues, incorporate feedback, and adapt to changing business environments effectively.

Additionally, ensuring employee compliance with handbook policies through education, communication, and enforcement mechanisms is crucial for maintaining a respectful, inclusive, and productive work environment while minimizing legal risks and liabilities.

Strategic Moves:

- **Handbook Reviews:** Regularly review the employee handbook to ensure it reflects the latest HR strategies, policies, and best practices.
- **Communication Protocols:** Reinforce communication protocols within the HR team, ensuring everyone is on the same page regarding key strategies and initiatives.

- **Continuous Improvement:** Encourage your team professionals to provide feedback on the handbook, fostering a culture of continuous improvement.

Energizing the HR Team

Just as players need the energy to perform at peak levels for the game, infusing energy into the HR team is imperative for boosting morale and motivation, ultimately driving productivity and engagement.

By fostering a positive and enthusiastic work atmosphere, you can inspire the team to approach challenges with creativity, resilience, and a can-do attitude. Regularly recognizing and celebrating achievements, both individual and collective, cultivates a sense of pride and accomplishment among team members.

Additionally, providing opportunities for professional growth, skill development, and empowerment encourages your team to take ownership of their roles and contribute meaningfully to organizational success.

Strategic Moves:

- **Motivational Sessions:** Conduct motivational sessions to inspire the HR team, emphasizing the impact of their work on the organization.
- **Recognition Programs:** Implement recognition programs to acknowledge outstanding HR contributions, reinforcing a positive and energized workplace culture.
- **Celebrating Success:** Celebrate HR successes and milestones, creating a sense of accomplishment and motivation for future endeavors.

Pregame techniques in HR set the stage for success by fostering team unity, aligning strategies with organizational goals, and supporting with preparing for challenges.

Play Calling Strategies: Orchestrating HR Success

Effective play calling is the key to navigating the complexities of the football game. Similarly, leveraging data-driven insights is essential for you and the HR team to make informed decisions in workforce management.

Leveraging Data-Driven Insights

Just as a football coach studies data to inform play calls, you and your team can analyze key metrics such as turnover rates, employee engagement scores, and key performance indicators, to identify trends, patterns, and areas for improvement. This data-driven approach enables you to develop targeted strategies and interventions to optimize initiatives effectively to drive success.

Strategic Moves:

- **HR Analytics:** Invest in HR analytics tools to gather and analyze relevant data, enabling fact-based decision-making.
- **Benchmarking:** Compare HR metrics and performance against industry benchmarks to identify areas for improvement.
- **Predictive Analytics:** Use predictive analytics to anticipate future workforce trends and proactively address potential challenges.

Adapting to Changing Workforce Dynamics

Football coaches adjust their plays based on the game's dynamics, and in today's rapidly changing workforce landscape, agility is crucial for you and your team to adapt HR strategies effectively. Being nimble allows for quick adjustments to meet emerging trends, technological advancements, and shifting employee preferences, ensuring continued relevance and effectiveness in talent management practices.

Strategic Moves:

- **Agile HR Practices:** Embrace agile HR methodologies that allow for flexibility and quick adjustments to changing workforce dynamics.

- **Continuous Learning:** Encourage your team to engage in continuous learning to stay abreast of industry trends and evolving workforce expectations.

- **Scenario Planning:** Develop scenario-based play-calling strategies to respond effectively to various workforce scenarios.

Tailoring HR Strategies for Different Situations

Football coaches have a variety of plays to choose from to support almost any scenario. Similarly, tailoring strategies to address specific HR challenges and opportunities is essential for achieving targeted outcomes and maximizing impact.

By customizing approaches based on the unique needs, dynamics, and goals of the company, you can effectively address pain points and capitalize on strengths within the workforce. This tailored approach enables HR to deploy resources more efficiently, allocate investments wisely, and prioritize initiatives that yield the greatest return on investment.

Strategic Moves:

- **Customized HR Solutions:** Develop customized HR solutions for specific workforce segments or departments, recognizing the needs within the organization.

- **Crisis Management Plans:** Establish crisis management plans with tailored responses for different types of HR crises.

- **Employee Lifecycle Strategies:** Implement different strategies for recruitment, onboarding, development, and retention, aligning with the varying stages of the employee lifecycle.

Collaborative Decision-Making

To execute a successful game drive, football plays that are executed often involve collaboration between coaches, players, and coordinators. Fostering a collaborative process between you and key stakeholders for decision-making is paramount for ensuring buy-in, alignment, and the success of HR initiatives.

By involving stakeholders from various departments, levels, and perspectives, you can tap into diverse expertise, insights, and experiences to inform strategic HR decisions effectively. This collaborative approach fosters transparency, trust, and engagement, empowering stakeholders to contribute ideas, voice concerns, and take ownership of outcomes.

Strategic Moves:

- **Cross-Functional Teams:** Form cross-functional HR teams to encourage collaboration and diverse perspectives in decision-making.
- **Decision-Making Frameworks:** Establish decision-making frameworks that involve input from various HR experts, ensuring well-rounded perspectives.
- **Communication Channels:** Facilitate open communication channels to gather insights and feedback from different HR team members.

Balancing Risk and Reward

Effective play calling in football requires a balance between evaluating the risk and the benefit of the reward. Assessing the risks and rewards of HR strategies is essential for informed decision-making and effective resource allocation. By conducting thorough risk assessments, you can identify potential pitfalls, anticipate challenges, and mitigate potential negative impacts on organizational performance.

Simultaneously, evaluating the rewards helps in recognizing opportunities, estimating potential benefits, and aligning HR initiatives with strategic objectives to maximize returns on investment.

Strategic Moves:

- **Risk Assessments:** Conduct thorough risk assessments for HR strategies, weighing potential risks against the anticipated rewards.

- **Innovation and Experimentation:** Encourage a culture of innovation and experimentation in HR, recognizing that calculated risks can lead to breakthroughs.

- **Continuous Evaluation:** Continuously evaluate the outcomes of HR strategies to adjust the play calling based on their success or challenges.

Play-calling strategies in HR involve leveraging data-driven insights, adapting to changing workforce dynamics, tailoring strategies for different situations, fostering collaborative decision-making, and balancing risk and reward. By mastering these strategies, you and your team can proactively manage success and navigate the human resources game with precision.

Real-Time Adaptation: Agility in HR Leadership

In football, the ability to adapt in real-time differentiates great teams from the rest. Similarly, the ability to navigate situations with real-time adaptation is a critical skill that empowers companies to thrive in a constantly changing landscape.

By staying agile and responsive, you can swiftly adjust strategies, processes, and resources to address emerging challenges and capitalize on new opportunities. This proactive approach fosters resilience, innovation, and competitiveness, enabling companies to maintain relevance and sustain growth amidst evolving market dynamics.

Embracing Change as a Constant

Embracing change and cultivating a mindset that thrives in dynamic environments is essential for you and your team to navigate challenges and seize opportunities effectively. By embracing change as an inevitable part of growth, you can foster resilience, agility, and adaptability within the team, enabling them to respond proactively to shifting circumstances.

Moreover, adopting a growth mindset encourages continuous learning, innovation, and experimentation, empowering team members to embrace challenges as opportunities for growth and development.

This proactive approach not only enhances individual and collective performance but also fosters a culture of creativity, collaboration, and forward-thinking within the organization.

Strategic Moves:

- **Change Management Training:** Provide training to HR teams on change management principles to cultivate an adaptable workforce.

- **Flexibility in Policies:** Design HR policies with flexibility, enabling quick adjustments to meet evolving organizational needs.

- **Communication Protocols:** Establish clear communication protocols to disseminate changes swiftly and ensure a unified response from the workforce.

Utilizing Real-Time Analytics

Football coaches analyze real-time game data to make instant decisions. Leveraging real-time analytics enables you to make data-driven decisions on workforce management with precision and agility. By harnessing insights from real-time data, you can identify trends, anticipate needs, and optimize strategies to maximize workforce productivity and performance. This proactive approach empowers you to stay ahead of challenges, capitalize on opportunities, and drive sustainable growth in today's dynamic business environment.

Strategic Moves:

- **Advanced HR Analytics Tools:** Invest in advanced HR analytics tools that provide real-time insights into workforce metrics.

- **Monitoring Key Performance Indicators (KPIs):** Identify and monitor critical HR KPIs in real-time to gauge the health of various HR functions.

- **Predictive Analytics for Trends:** Utilize predictive analytics to anticipate emerging trends and address issues before they escalate.

Agile Policy Adjustments

Just as football coaches adjust their game plan during a game, being prepared to make policy adjustments allows you to promptly address immediate needs and adapt to evolving circumstances within the organization. Flexibility in policymaking ensures that you can respond effectively to changing dynamics, mitigate risks, and maintain alignment with organizational goals and priorities.

Strategic Moves:

- **Policy Flexibility:** Design HR policies with built-in flexibility, allowing for quick adjustments based on changing circumstances.

- **Crisis Response Teams:** Establish crisis response teams that can rapidly assess situations and recommend immediate policy adaptations.

- **Communication Channels:** Ensure that employees are informed promptly about policy changes through effective communication channels.

Rapid Decision-Making Protocols

In the heat of a football game, split-second decisions can be game-changers that can determine whether the team wins or loses the game. Establishing rapid decision-making protocols for critical situations is paramount to ensure swift and effective responses when facing unexpected challenges.

By implementing clear procedures and empowering key

stakeholders to make timely decisions, you can minimize disruptions, mitigate risks, and maintain organizational resilience in times of uncertainty.

Strategic Moves:

- **Decision-Making Frameworks:** Develop clear decision-making frameworks that guide your team in rapidly assessing and responding to urgent matters.
- **Emergency Response Training:** Conduct training sessions to prepare HR teams for rapid decision-making during crises.
- **Simulation Exercises:** Engage in simulated exercises that mimic real-time scenarios, allowing HR professionals to practice swift decision-making.

Continuous Learning Culture

Real-time adaptation requires a culture of continuous learning. Fostering an environment where teams are encouraged to learn and adapt on the fly cultivates agility, innovation, and resilience within the team. By empowering your team to embrace change and continuously improve their processes, you can enhance problem-solving abilities, drive efficiency, and stay competitive in today's fast-paced business landscape.

Strategic Moves:

- **Continuous Training Programs:** Implement ongoing training programs that keep HR professionals abreast of industry trends and emerging practices.
- **Knowledge Sharing Platforms:** Establish platforms for knowledge sharing and collaborative learning within the HR team.
- **Post-Event Reviews:** Conduct post-event reviews to extract lessons learned and identify areas for improvement in real-time adaptation strategies.

Real-time adaptation in HR leadership involves embracing change as a constant, utilizing real-time analytics, making agile policy adjustments, establishing rapid decision-making protocols, and fostering a continuous learning culture. By mastering these strategies, you will empower your team to achieve success.

Halftime Adjustments: Pivoting for HR Success

The best football coaches make halftime adjustments that turn the balance of a football game. Similarly, mastering the art of making adjustments is crucial for leading your team toward success in dynamic environments. By recognizing the need for adaptation and swiftly pivoting strategies, you can effectively navigate challenges and seize emerging opportunities.

This ability to pivot enables you to stay agile, responsive, and proactive in addressing evolving needs and market shifts. Moreover, by fostering a culture of flexibility and innovation, you empower your team to embrace change and capitalize on new possibilities. Ultimately, mastering the art of adjusting allows you to propel your team toward success by leveraging their talents, resources, and collective strengths to achieve strategic objectives.

Embracing change as a catalyst for growth, you can lead your team to overcome obstacles, drive performance, and achieve sustainable results in today's ever-changing business landscape.

Reflecting on First-Half Performance

Halftime provides the football team with a moment for reflection and assessment. Taking time to analyze first-half performance is crucial for identifying strengths and pinpointing areas that require adjustment to optimize team performance. By conducting a thorough review, you can leverage strengths, address weaknesses, and develop a strategic plan to propel the team toward success in the second half.

Strategic Moves:

- **Performance Metrics Review:** Evaluate HR performance metrics from the first half, including talent acquisition, employee engagement, and compliance.

- **Feedback Sessions:** Conduct feedback sessions with HR teams to gather insights on challenges and successes.

- **Identify Quick Wins:** Identify quick wins that can be leveraged for immediate impact in the second half.

Tactical Reevaluation of Strategies

Tactical reevaluation of strategies involves critically assessing the effectiveness of current approaches and adjusting as needed to achieve desired outcomes. By analyzing key performance indicators and market dynamics, your team can identify areas for improvement and refine their tactics to stay agile and competitive.

Strategic Moves:

- **SWOT Analysis:** Conduct a quick SWOT analysis to reassess strengths, weaknesses, opportunities, and threats.

- **Benchmarking Against Competitors:** Benchmark HR strategies against industry competitors to identify areas for improvement.

- **Incorporate Market Trends:** Integrate emerging market trends into HR strategies for enhanced relevance.

Dynamic Workforce Planning

Halftime adjustments often involve reshuffling players for optimal performance. HR leaders should engage in dynamic workforce planning, ensuring the right talents are in the right positions for the second-half challenges.

Strategic Moves:

- **Skill Alignment:** Reevaluate employee skills and competencies, ensuring alignment with organizational goals.

- **Talent Redistribution:** Consider redistributing talents within teams to address skill gaps and maximize efficiency.

- **Succession Planning:** Initiate or review succession planning strategies to ensure continuity in key roles.

Communication Enhancement

Halftime is a critical timeframe for coaches to communicate adjustments to players. Enhancing communication strategies is essential to ensure that the entire team is aligned with future plans and organizational goals. By fostering transparent and open channels of communication, you can promote clarity, collaboration, and shared understanding among team members.

Additionally, effective communication facilitates the dissemination of information, promotes engagement, and builds trust within the team, empowering individuals to contribute effectively toward common objectives.

Strategic Moves:

- **Clear Communication Channels:** Strengthen communication channels to ensure timely dissemination of information.

- **Employee Feedback Platforms:** Implement or refine platforms for collecting employee feedback on HR initiatives.

- **Town Hall Meetings:** Conduct town hall meetings to transparently communicate adjustments and updates.

Agile Problem-Solving

Adaptability is key during halftime adjustments. Cultivating an agile problem-solving mindset within your team is essential for effectively addressing unforeseen challenges and seizing emerging opportunities. By encouraging flexibility, creativity, and adaptability, you empower team members to respond swiftly and resourcefully to changing circumstances. Moreover, fostering an environment where experimentation and learning are valued enables the team to innovate and develop effective solutions in dynamic situations.

Strategic Moves:

- **Agile Training Programs:** Implement agile training programs to enhance problem-solving skills within HR teams.

- **Scenario-Based Workshops:** Conduct scenario-based workshops to prepare HR professionals for unexpected challenges.

- **Cross-Functional Collaboration:** Encourage cross-functional collaboration for collective problem-solving.

By mastering these halftime strategies, you and your team will be better equipped to adapt, refine tactics, and overcome challenges in the second half. This proactive approach ensures readiness to capitalize on opportunities and drive performance toward achieving strategic objectives.

Post-Game Analysis: Extracting Insights for Future Wins

A post-game analysis in football is important for refining strategies and improving performance. As the second half concludes, HR leaders must also conduct a comprehensive post-game analysis to extract valuable insights, learn from experiences, and adjust game plans for the future to ensure success.

Evaluation of Second-Half Performance

Executing a detailed evaluation of performance is instrumental in understanding what worked well and what needs improvement. By analyzing key metrics and outcomes, you can identify strengths to leverage and areas for enhancement. This process will enable your team to make informed decisions, refine strategies, and optimize performance for greater success in future endeavors.

Strategic Moves:

- **Metrics Review:** Scrutinize HR metrics related to talent management, employee satisfaction, and goal attainment.

- **Post-Implementation Review:** Assess the impact of HR initiatives implemented in the second half.

- **Employee Feedback Analysis:** Analyze post-game feedback from employees to gauge the effectiveness of HR strategies.

Lessons Learned and Best Practices

A successful post-game analysis involves extracting lessons learned and identifying best practices that can be replicated in future scenarios. Focusing on distilling valuable insights from both successes and challenges enables your team to glean actionable lessons and adapt accordingly. By analyzing the factors contributing to both positive outcomes and setbacks, you gain a comprehensive understanding of what drives success and where improvements are needed. This strategic approach empowers your team to refine strategies, optimize processes, and foster continuous improvement, ultimately enhancing overall performance and achieving long-term goals.

Strategic Moves:

- **Best Practices Documentation:** Document successful HR strategies and practices for future reference.
- **Lessons Learned Sessions:** Conduct sessions with your team to discuss and internalize lessons learned.
- **Benchmark Against Industry Standards:** Compare HR practices against industry benchmarks to identify areas of improvement.

Continuous Improvement Initiatives

The post-game analysis serves as a foundation for continuous improvement. Leveraging the insights gained allows you and your team to refine existing processes, enhance capabilities, and implement changes that drive ongoing success. By applying lessons learned from past experiences, you can optimize efficiency, mitigate risks, and adapt strategies to evolving circumstances.

Strategic Moves:

- **Process Refinement:** Identify opportunities for streamlining HR processes based on post-game insights.

- **Training and Development Plans:** Develop targeted training and development plans for the team.
- **Technology Upgrades:** Assess the need for technology upgrades or enhancements based on post-game requirements.

Celebrating Wins and Recognizing Contributions

Acknowledging victories and recognizing the contributions of HR teams is an essential aspect of post-game analysis. Fostering a culture of celebration and appreciation is crucial for boosting morale and motivation within your team. Recognizing achievements, milestones, and contributions cultivates a sense of value and belonging among team members.

By expressing gratitude and acknowledging efforts, you reinforce positive behaviors and encourage continued dedication to shared goals.

Ultimately, a culture of celebration fosters a supportive and uplifting work environment, driving engagement and performance across the organization.

Strategic Moves:

- **Recognition Programs:** Implement employee recognition programs to acknowledge outstanding HR contributions.
- **Team Celebrations:** Organize team-building events and celebrations to foster camaraderie.
- **Highlight Achievements:** Share HR achievements with the broader organization to showcase the department's impact.

Strategic Planning for the Next Game

The post-game analysis sets the stage for strategic planning for the next game. Using the insights gained, you can adjust your playbook, set new goals, and align HR strategies with organizational needs.

By analyzing data and feedback, you gain valuable information to inform strategic decisions and refine approaches. This proactive adjustment ensures that HR initiatives remain agile and responsive to evolving circumstances, maximizing their effectiveness in supporting overall business objectives. Ultimately, leveraging insights to adapt strategies fosters continuous improvement and enhances the HR team's ability to drive positive outcomes for the organization.

Strategic Moves:

- **Playbook Adjustments:** Modify the HR playbook based on post-game analysis findings.

- **Goal Setting:** Establish new HR goals and objectives aligned with organizational priorities.

- **Alignment with Organizational Changes:** Ensure HR strategies are adaptable to any changes in the overall organizational strategy.

A comprehensive post-game analysis in HR involves evaluating performance, documenting lessons learned, driving continuous improvement, celebrating wins, and strategically planning for the next game. By incorporating these strategic moves into the post-game analysis, you continue to pave the way for ongoing success.

CHAPTER **5**

Leading from the Sidelines

✓ Strategic Timeout: Reassessing, Refocusing, and Realigning
✓ Inspirational Coaching: Motivating HR Teams toward Excellence
✓ Sideline Communication: Navigating HR Initiatives with Precision
✓ Crisis Management: Navigating the Storms with Resilience
✓ Touchdown Celebrations: Acknowledging HR Wins with Finesse

Strategic Timeout: Reassessing, Refocusing, and Realigning

The ability to call a timeout anytime during gameplay play provides you and your team the opportunity to reflect, recalibrate, and re-focus. As the CHRO, envision this chapter as your timeout, where you bring the team together in the huddle to reevaluate the game plan and decide on whether a new course is charted.

Bill Walsh, coach of the Super Bowl Champion San Francisco 49ers once said, "The score takes care of itself when you take care of the details."

This chapter covers the tactic of executing strategic timeouts. The timeframe called to reassess, refocus, and realign your HR strategies.

Evaluating Current HR Strategies

A strategic timeout offers you an opportunity to step back and evaluate the effectiveness of current strategies. During this reflective period, reassessing existing approaches helps pinpoint areas for refinement and innovation. By taking this proactive step, your team can adjust its tactics to better align with organizational goals and address and/or improve any identified challenges.

Strategic Moves:

- **Initiative Assessment:** Evaluate the progress of major HR initiatives in terms of goals, objectives, and outcomes.
- **KPI Review:** Analyze key performance indicators to measure the impact of HR strategies.
- **Organizational Alignment:** Assess how well HR strategies align with the current organizational landscape.

Identifying Pain Points and Challenges

By assessing pain points and challenges, it becomes possible to pinpoint areas requiring improvement and to foresee potential roadblocks ahead. This analytical approach empowers you to make informed decisions about adjusting strategies or implementing new approaches to overcome identified obstacles.

Additionally, taking the time to evaluate current initiatives fosters a culture of continuous improvement within your team, ensuring that efforts are consistently optimized to meet evolving organizational needs.

Ultimately, leveraging the timeout to assess and address challenges enhances the team's agility and resilience, positioning them for greater success in achieving their objectives.

Strategic Moves:

- **Stakeholder Feedback:** Gather feedback from key stakeholders on HR processes and initiatives.
- **Employee Input:** Solicit input from employees to identify challenges they may be facing.
- **SWOT Analysis:** Conduct a brief SWOT analysis to identify internal strengths and weaknesses.

Adjusting the Playbook for Optimal Results

Just as a football coach may adjust their playbook during a timeout, HR leaders should use this pause to make necessary adjustments to their strategic playbook. This may involve refining existing strategies, introducing innovative approaches, or realigning priorities.

Strategic Moves:

- **Playbook Adjustments:** Modify HR strategies based on the insights gained.
- **Innovation Injection:** Introduce innovative practices or technologies to enhance HR efficiency.
- **Priority Realignment:** Reassess priorities and realign HR efforts with the most critical organizational needs.

Employee and Stakeholder Engagement

Engaging with employees and key stakeholders is crucial during the strategic timeout. You and your team should communicate openly, address concerns, and seek input to ensure that the HR strategies are well-understood and supported across the organization.

Strategic Moves:

- **Town Hall Meetings:** Conduct town hall meetings to communicate HR strategies and gather feedback.
- **Open Door Policy:** Reinforce an open-door policy for employees to share their thoughts and concerns.
- **Stakeholder Collaboration:** Collaborate with key stakeholders to ensure their alignment with HR strategies.

Goal Refinement and Reenergizing the Team

As the strategic timeout concludes, you should refine your teams' goals based on the insights gained and reenergize the HR team for the next phase of execution. This involves setting clear objectives, inspiring the team, and fostering a renewed sense of purpose.

Strategic Moves:

- **Goal Refinement:** Clarify and refine HR goals based on the strategic timeout assessment.
- **Team Motivation:** Implement motivational initiatives to reenergize the HR team.
- **Communicate Adjustments:** Engage and openly communicate any adjustments to HR strategies and goals.

A strategic timeout in HR provides a crucial moment to evaluate current strategies, address challenges, adjust the playbook, engage stakeholders, and reenergize the team. By incorporating these strategic moves during the timeout, you ensure your team is poised for success in the next phases of strategic planning and execution.

Inspirational Coaching: Motivating HR Teams Toward Excellence

As the Chief Human Resources Officer (CHRO), one of the pivotal roles you play is that of an inspirational coach, driving your team towards excellence and pushing boundaries. Your ability to motivate and empower your team members goes beyond mere encouragement; it's about instilling a sense of purpose and passion for their work.

By setting high standards and fostering a culture of accountability, you challenge your team to strive for success beyond what is conventionally expected. Through your leadership, you cultivate an environment where innovation thrives, and individuals feel empowered to explore new ideas and approaches.

Your unwavering commitment to excellence serves as a guiding light, inspiring your team to surpass their limitations and achieve remarkable results. By fostering a growth mindset and emphasizing the importance of continuous improvement, you instill confidence in your team's abilities and encourage them to embrace challenges as opportunities for growth.

Ultimately, your role as an inspirational coach is not just about achieving short-term goals; it's about nurturing a culture of excellence that drives sustained success and propels your organization toward its long-term vision.

Understanding the Power of Inspiration

Like a coach rallying their players before a game, you must inspire confidence, foster a positive mindset, and drive a shared sense of purpose. Understanding the role of the inspirational coach includes providing motivation and encouragement to your team. By embodying this role effectively, you can inspire your team members to push their limits and achieve their full potential. The impact of serving as an inspirational coach extends beyond immediate results, fostering a culture of excellence and empowerment within your team.

Coaching Dynamics:

- **Motivational Leadership:** Embrace a leadership style that motivates and inspires your team.
  - Styles include: 1) Transformational leaders inspire and motivate followers by setting high expectations and encouraging innovation and change. 2) Servant leaders prioritize the needs of their team members, focusing on their growth and development while fostering a sense of community and collaboration. 3) Charismatic leaders use their personal charm and charisma to inspire and energize others, often by articulating a compelling vision and leading by example. Each style has its unique approach to motivation, but all aim to inspire and empower followers to achieve their goals.

- **Positive Reinforcement:** Recognize and reinforce positive behaviors and contributions.
- **Shared Vision:** Communicate a compelling vision that resonates with the HR team.

Building a Culture of Excellence

Just as a football coach cultivates a culture of excellence within their team, success is achieved when you prioritize and foster an environment where excellence is not only encouraged but becomes a natural part of the organizational DNA.

Cultural Elements:

- **High Standards:** Set and communicate high standards for performance and professionalism.
- **Continuous Improvement:** Encourage a mindset of continuous learning and improvement.
- **Recognition Programs:** Implement programs to acknowledge and celebrate excellence.

Empowering HR Team Members

Empowering your HR team to realize their full potential involves providing them with opportunities for growth, autonomy, and recognition. By fostering an environment of trust and support, your team will have the opportunity to unleash their creativity and expertise to drive impactful change within the organization. Additionally, empowerment provides the necessary tools, resources, and support to enable each team member to contribute to the overall success of the HR function.

Empowerment Strategies:

- **Skill Development:** Offer opportunities for skill development and professional growth.
- **Autonomy and Responsibility:** Delegate responsibilities, granting team members a sense of ownership.
- **Supportive Environment:** Create a supportive environment where team members feel valued and heard.

Effective Communication and Feedback

Communication is a cornerstone of coaching. Effective communication of goals, expectations, and feedback is paramount in fostering a culture of transparency and trust within the HR team. By providing mentorship and encouraging open dialogue, you create an environment where team members feel valued, empowered, and motivated to contribute their best. This collaborative approach not only enhances teamwork and productivity but also cultivates a sense of ownership and accountability toward achieving organizational objectives.

Communication Tactics:

- **Clear Goal Communication:** Articulate clear goals and expectations for HR team members.
- **Feedback Mechanisms:** Establish regular feedback sessions to guide and support individual growth.

- **Celebrating Achievements:** Communicate successes and milestones to inspire collective pride.

Nurturing Resilience and Tenacity

Inspirational coaching involves nurturing resilience within the HR team, much like a football coach instills resilience in their players to overcome challenges and setbacks.

Resilience-Building Strategies:

- **Learning from Setbacks:** Encourage a mindset that views setbacks as opportunities for growth.
- **Crisis Management Training:** Provide training on handling crises and challenges effectively.
- **Team Bonding:** Foster a sense of camaraderie that strengthens the team during tough times.

Being an inspirational coach is such an important aspect of your role, and involves understanding the power of motivation, fostering a culture of excellence, empowering team members through effective communication, and nurturing resilience.

Sideline Communication: Navigating HR Initiatives with Precision

Navigating HR initiatives with precision requires clear communication, ensuring that key messages are effectively conveyed to all stakeholders. By fostering engagement and soliciting feedback, HR leaders can ensure that plans are executed with precision, aligning with organizational goals and objectives. This approach not only enhances transparency and accountability but also fosters a culture of collaboration and continuous improvement within the HR team.

The Importance of Sideline Communication

Football coaches relay critical information to players on the field throughout the game to ensure clarity of direction and/or key changes to the plan. As the CHRO, prioritizing communication is paramount to ensure that information flows seamlessly within the team and across the organization. Mastering the art of communication involves not only delivering messages effectively but also actively listening to feedback and addressing concerns in real time.

Real-Time Updates:

- **Timely Information Sharing:** Develop systems for real-time sharing of critical information and updates.
- **Emergency Response:** Establish protocols for immediate communication during HR emergencies.
- **Centralized Communication Hub:** Create a centralized platform for quick dissemination of information.

Precision in Messaging

Sideline communication involves delivering messages with clarity and ensuring that every member of the HR team understands their role and the broader objectives. Precision in messaging prevents misinterpretation and aligns everyone with the overall strategy.

Message Clarity:

- **Strategic Alignment:** Clearly articulate how individual tasks align with the broader HR strategy.
- **Expectation Setting:** Set clear expectations for timelines, goals, and performance metrics.
- **Adaptability:** Ensure messages are adaptable to different audience segments within the HR team.

Technology as a Sideline Tool

In the game of football, technology has greatly enhanced the primary method of communication between coaches and players. From using tablets to review game plans and plays in real-time during a game, to the 30-second open microphone allowing the coach to communicate the play to the quarterback before the team lines up at the ball.

In today's digital age, leveraging modern communication tools is essential for you to set a new standard, streamline interactions, and enhance collaboration within your team. These tools not only eliminate the inefficiencies associated with email version control but also provide a centralized platform for real-time communication and document sharing.

Technology Integration:

- **Collaboration Platforms:** Utilize collaboration tools for seamless communication and document sharing.
- **Video Conferencing:** Implement mandates for video conferencing (with the camera on) to support face-to-face communication.
- **Mobile Accessibility:** Ensure communication tools are accessible via mobile devices for those traveling.

Collaboration and Coordination

Sideline communication in HR involves fostering collaboration and coordination among team members. Collaboration and coordination are vital aspects of HR management, requiring synchronization among team members for optimal performance. When HR professionals work together seamlessly, they can leverage their collective expertise to tackle challenges more effectively and achieve organizational objectives efficiently.

By fostering a culture of collaboration and ensuring coordination across various HR functions, teams can enhance productivity, drive innovation, and deliver high-quality outcomes.

Team Coordination:

- **Cross-functional collaboration:** Encourage collaboration across different HR functions for holistic planning.
- **Regular Check-Ins:** Schedule regular check-ins to assess progress and address any challenges.
- **Task Allocation:** Clearly define roles and responsibilities to avoid duplication and confusion.

Crisis Management and Decision-Making

Communication, transparency, and engagement are crucial during crises, requiring you and your team to make swift decisions. Effective communication channels aid in crisis management and enable quick decision-making to address unexpected challenges.

Crisis Communication Protocols:

- **Pre-Defined Communication Plans:** Establish pre-defined protocols and plans for communicating during crises.
- **Decision-Making Framework:** Develop a framework for quick decision-making in high-pressure situations.
- **Transparency:** Communicate transparently about challenges and potential solutions.

Prioritizing and driving effective communications during crisis management is crucial for ensuring timely and accurate dissemination of information. By leveraging technology, HR teams can streamline communication channels, enabling swift updates and instructions to be relayed to employees, stakeholders, and the broader community.

Crisis Management: Navigating the Storms with Resilience

In the game of HR leadership, the ability to weather crises is a defining factor of your leadership. Like a football team facing unexpected challenges and adjusting the game plan to compensate for the challenges, effective crisis management is key to ensuring organizational resilience and long-term success.

The Nature of HR Storms

Crisis management involves navigating unforeseen challenges (layoffs, leadership changes, legal issues, payroll disruptions, etc.) that can impact the organization's workforce, culture, and overall well-being. Being prepared for disruptions and adapting to steer your team through uncertainty requires a proactive approach to risk management and contingency planning. By anticipating potential challenges and developing flexible strategies, you and your team can effectively navigate unexpected events and maintain business continuity.

Identifying HR Storms:

- **Anticipate Challenges:** Develop foresight to identify potential crises and overall impacts to the organization.
- **Scenario Planning:** Conduct scenario planning exercises to prepare for various crisis scenarios.
- **Continuous Monitoring:** Implement systems for continuous monitoring of internal and external factors.

Establishing Crisis Response Protocols

Similarly to a football team having a playbook for various game scenarios, you and your team need well-defined crisis response protocols. These protocols serve as a guide for managing different types of crises efficiently.

Crisis Response Playbook:

- **Pre-defined protocols:** Establish clear protocols for addressing common HR crises, such as layoffs, legal issues, or cultural challenges.
- **Team Roles and Responsibilities:** Define roles and responsibilities within the HR team during a crisis.
- **Communication Strategies:** Develop communication strategies tailored to different crisis scenarios.

Communication in Crisis

Just as a quarterback communicates plays amid chaos, HR leaders must convey information with clarity, transparency, and empathy during turbulent times.

Transparent Communication:

- **Timely Updates:** Provide regular and timely updates to all stakeholders.

- **Empathy and Assurance:** Communicate with empathy, assuring employees and stakeholders that the situation is being addressed.

- **Clear Guidance:** Offer clear guidance on what is expected from employees and the organization during the crisis.

Decisive Decision-Making

The importance of being prepared to make decisive decisions lies in the ability to act swiftly and effectively in response to evolving situations. By having a clear understanding of priorities and potential outcomes, you can navigate challenges with confidence and lead your team toward successful outcomes.

Decision-Making Agility:

- **Assessing Options:** Evaluate various options and their potential consequences.

- **Prioritizing Impact:** Prioritize decisions based on their impact on employees, culture, and the overall organization.

- **Adaptability:** Remain adaptable and open to adjusting strategies as the crisis unfolds.

Learning and Adapting

After weathering a crisis, HR leaders must engage in post-crisis analysis, learning from the experience to enhance future crisis management capabilities.

Post-Crisis Evaluation:

- **Debriefing Sessions:** Conduct debriefing sessions to assess the effectiveness of crisis response strategies.
- **Continuous Improvement:** Identify areas for improvement and update crisis response protocols accordingly.
- **Building Resilience:** Use crisis experiences to build resilience within the HR team and the organization.

Just as a football team emerges stronger after facing adversity, CHROs who master crisis management contribute to the resilience and long-term success of their organizations.

Touchdown Celebrations: Acknowledging HR Wins with Finesse

Just like a well-executed touchdown celebration in football can be found on YouTube, Instagram, X, and ESPN, acknowledging accomplishments with flair is vital for boosting morale and fostering a culture of recognition within the organization. It not only celebrates individual and team achievements but also inspires others to strive for excellence.

By publicly recognizing success, you reinforce positive behaviors and encourage continued effort and dedication. Moreover, celebrating accomplishments creates a sense of pride and camaraderie among employees, enhancing overall satisfaction and engagement.

Celebrating HR Victories

Touchdown celebrations are all about recognizing and appreciating the achievements of the team and the organization. Just as a football team jumps for joy when scoring a touchdown, HR leaders should create a culture where victories are openly celebrated and shared.

Recognition Culture:

- **Employee Acknowledgment:** Recognize the efforts of individual employees and teams for their exceptional contributions.
- **Public Celebrations:** Conduct public celebrations, whether virtual or in-person, to spotlight major achievements.
- **Leadership Recognition:** Acknowledge the leadership team's role in steering the organization toward success.

Fostering a Positive Atmosphere

Touchdown celebrations contribute to the positive atmosphere within a football team. Similarly, fostering a positive atmosphere is essential for integrating employee recognition into the organizational culture. By consistently acknowledging and celebrating employee contributions, you reinforce the value of recognition and inspire others to embrace a culture of appreciation and acknowledgment.

Positive Reinforcement:

- **Boosting Morale:** Celebrate wins to boost employee morale and motivation.
- **Cultivating Team Spirit:** Use celebrations as a means to strengthen the sense of unity and collaboration among team members.
- **Creating Positive Memories:** Build a reservoir of positive memories by attaching celebratory moments to major accomplishments.

Tailoring Celebrations to Achievements

No two touchdown celebrations are the same. You and your team should customize acknowledgment strategies based on the nature and significance of the achievement.

Tailored Acknowledgments:

- **Varied Recognition Methods:** Utilize diverse recognition methods, such as awards, shout-outs, or team events, depending on the nature of the achievement.

- **Personalized Appreciation:** Personalize acknowledgment to make individuals feel valued for their unique contributions.

- **Flexibility:** Be flexible in the approach, ensuring that celebrations align with the organizational culture, and most importantly, involve those being recognized and/or celebrated.

Showcasing Organizational Success

Showcasing organizational success by spotlighting the collective effort of the team is crucial for fostering a sense of unity and pride within the organization. By highlighting the collaborative achievements of individuals and teams, you not only recognize their hard work but also reinforce the idea that success is a result of collective effort and teamwork.

Organizational Milestones:

- **Highlighting Team Contributions:** Emphasize the collaborative efforts of all of the teams that led to the achievement.

- **Inclusive Celebrations:** Ensure that celebrations involve the entire organization, fostering a sense of shared success.

- **Broadcasting Success Stories:** Share success stories to inspire and motivate employees at all levels.

Sustaining Momentum

The excitement of a touchdown celebration captured on camera resonates long after the game and often goes viral on X, Instagram, and YouTube. Sustaining momentum after a win involves leveraging the positive energy generated by achievements.

Building on Success:

- **Strategic Planning:** Use celebratory moments as catalysts for strategic planning and future initiatives.

- **Continuous Improvement:** Encourage a mindset of continuous improvement, leveraging victories as stepping stones for greater success.

- **Employee Engagement:** Channel the positive energy from celebrations into ongoing employee engagement efforts.

Just as a memorable touchdown celebration adds excitement to a football game, individual and team recognition adds vitality to the organizational culture.

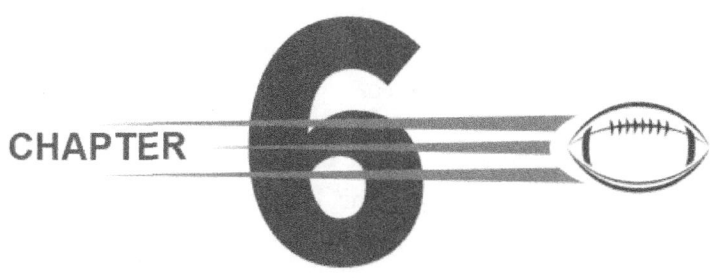

CHAPTER **6**

Building Endurance for the Long Season

- ✓ Endurance Training: Building the Stamina for HR Excellence
- ✓ Resilience in Adversity: Weathering the Storms of HR Leadership
- ✓ Managing the HR Season: Sustaining Performance for the Long Haul
- ✓ Strategy for HR Success: Optimizing Performance through Phases
- ✓ Celebrating Milestones

Endurance Training: Building the Stamina for HR Excellence

Endurance training in HR involves consistently honing skills, staying updated with industry trends, and maintaining resilience in the face of challenges. By prioritizing endurance training, you can build the stamina needed to excel, navigate complexities, and drive organizational success over the long term.

Hall of Fame coach Jimmy Johnson, and back-to-back Super Bowl-winner for the Dallas Cowboys has a formula for success: Positive Attitude + Effort = Performance.

As the CHRO, building endurance is about embracing opportunities to strengthen your leadership. This chapter highlights techniques to lead the HR function with resilience, ensuring your strategies stand the test of time with consistent victories.

Enduring overtime in the HR game

Endurance in HR is like a football team being prepared mentally and physically for the game going into overtime during 100-degree weather. It involves preparing for the long haul, anticipating obstacles, and equipping the team with the resilience needed to overcome the inevitable challenges.

Strategic Planning:

- **Long-Term Vision:** Develop a long-term vision, or ambitions plan, for HR initiatives, aligning them with the organization's strategic goals.
- **Roadmap for Success:** Create a roadmap that extends beyond immediate challenges, outlining a path for sustained success.
- **Scenario Planning:** Anticipate potential obstacles and devise contingency plans for navigation.

Building Resilience in HR Leaders

Just as endurance training strengthens an athlete's resilience, building resilience in HR leaders involves cultivating a mindset that embraces setbacks as opportunities for growth and development. By fostering resilience, HR leaders can effectively navigate challenges, bounce back from setbacks, and lead their teams with confidence and adaptability.

Emotional Intelligence:

- **Coping Mechanisms:** Develop effective coping mechanisms to handle stress and pressure.
- **Adaptability:** Cultivate adaptability to navigate unforeseen challenges with composure.
- **Learning from Setbacks:** View setbacks as opportunities for growth, learning, and improvement.

Sustaining Energy and Momentum

Endurance training is about sustaining energy levels throughout a prolonged effort. Sustaining energy and momentum in HR initiatives is vital to maintaining enthusiasm and drive among team members amidst ongoing projects. By proactively managing workload and providing support, HR leaders can keep the team motivated and focused on achieving organizational goals.

Employee Engagement:

- **Continuous Motivation:** Implement strategies to keep employees motivated and engaged in long-term projects.
- **Feedback Loops:** Establish feedback loops to assess and enhance team morale and energy levels.
- **Recognition:** Recognize and celebrate small wins to fuel ongoing enthusiasm.

Strategic Resource Allocation

Endurance training involves allocating resources efficiently for sustained performance. Strategic resource allocation is essential for prolonged success in HR, ensuring that resources are optimally utilized to meet both short-term and long-term objectives. By aligning resources with strategic priorities and regularly reassessing team competencies and allocation strategies, you can sustain success and adapt to changing organizational needs over time.

Resource Management:

- **Budget Planning:** Develop a comprehensive HR budget that aligns with long-term goals.
- **Talent Allocation:** Strategically allocate talent and skills for maximum impact on ongoing and future projects.
- **Technology Investment:** Invest in technology that supports innovating HR strategies and adapts to evolving needs.

Cultivating Team Endurance

Endurance is not only an individual pursuit but a collective effort. Cultivating team endurance involves fostering a sense of unity and cohesion among team members, encouraging mutual support and collaboration to withstand challenges together. By promoting a culture of resilience and perseverance, teams can navigate obstacles more effectively and emerge stronger from adversity. Strong leadership and open communication are key to maintaining team morale and motivation during challenging times, fostering a resilient spirit that propels the team forward.

Team Building:

- **Collaborative Culture:** Nurture a collaborative culture where team members support each other through the ups and downs.
- **Communication:** Establish open lines of communication to address challenges collectively and celebrate successes.

- **Training and Development:** Invest in ongoing training to enhance the collective skills and capabilities of the HR team.

Celebrating Milestones in the Marathon

Just as a football team likely celebrates a double overtime win in a more unique way than a win accomplished during regulation, celebrating milestones is essential for recognizing significant achievements and fostering a sense of accomplishment within the team. It provides an opportunity to acknowledge individual and collective efforts, boosting morale and motivation. By commemorating milestones, organizations reinforce their appreciation for hard work and dedication, fueling enthusiasm for future endeavors.

Strategic Milestones:

- **Periodic Reviews:** Conduct periodic reviews to assess progress toward long-term goals.
- **Acknowledgment:** Celebrate significant achievements and milestones as markers of progress.
- **Adaptation:** Use milestone celebrations as opportunities to adapt and refine strategies for the journey ahead.

Endurance training in HR is not just about surviving; it's about thriving over the long haul. By applying these techniques, you equip yourself and your team with the skillsets and motivation to excel in the enduring marathon of human resources leadership.

Resilience in Adversity: Weathering the Storms of HR Leadership

In the face of adversity, resiliency becomes the anchor that keeps HR leadership steady. Just as a football team withstands storms on and off the field, HR leaders must develop the fortitude to navigate challenges, adapt to change, and emerge stronger.

Understanding Adversity in HR Leadership

Adversity in HR is inevitable, whether it's managing crises, navigating organizational changes, or addressing employee challenges. Resilience in this context involves the ability to face adversity head-on and transform setbacks into opportunities.

Adapting to Change:

- **Agile Mindset:** Cultivate an agile mindset to adapt swiftly to changing circumstances.
- **Change Management Strategies:** Develop robust change management strategies to guide the team through transitions.
- **Learning Orientation:** Encourage a learning orientation that views adversity as a chance for growth and improvement.

Building Individual Resilience

Just as football players train to withstand the physical demands of the game, building resilience is crucial for HR leaders to navigate the challenges and uncertainties inherent in their roles. It enables them to bounce back from setbacks, maintain focus, and lead effectively even in the face of adversity.

Stress Management:

- **Creative Techniques:** Introduce creative techniques to manage stress and maintain focus.
- **Self-Care Practices:** Promote self-care practices to recharge and maintain mental and emotional well-being.
- **Seeking Support:** Encourage a culture where seeking support is seen as a strength, not a weakness.

Fostering Team Resilience

The collective resilience of the team is crucial for navigating challenges together and maintaining a cohesive unit. Fostering team resilience involves creating a supportive environment where team members feel valued, empowered, and encouraged to overcome obstacles together.

Team Cohesion:

- **Open Communication:** Foster an environment of open communication where team members can share concerns and ideas.
- **Collaborative Problem-Solving:** Encourage collaborative problem-solving to harness the collective intelligence of the team.
- **Mutual Support:** Cultivate a culture of mutual support, where team members rally together during challenging times.

Strategic Decision-Making in Adversity

Strategic decision-making in adversity demands a careful balance of agility and foresight, allowing you to navigate uncertainties while staying focused on long-term goals. It involves evaluating risks, leveraging available resources effectively, and adapting strategies to changing circumstances to steer the organization toward success despite challenges.

Risk Mitigation:

- **Scenario Planning:** Engage in scenario planning to anticipate potential challenges and devise mitigation strategies.
- **Decision Agility:** Develop decision-making agility to make informed choices in rapidly changing situations.
- **Learning from Setbacks:** Treat setbacks as opportunities to refine strategies and improve future decision-making.

Embracing a Growth Mindset

Embracing a growth mindset with resilience involves acknowledging setbacks as learning opportunities and remaining adaptable to change. It requires a commitment to continuous improvement, where challenges are seen as stepping stones toward personal and professional development. Leaders who cultivate a growth mindset encourage their teams to embrace challenges, persist in the face of adversity, and view failures as valuable lessons on the path to success.

Continuous Learning:

- **Learning Culture:** Instill a culture of continuous learning where every challenge is an opportunity to acquire new skills and insights.
- **Innovation:** Encourage innovative thinking to find creative solutions in the face of adversity.
- **Celebrating Resilience:** Recognize and celebrate instances of resilience within the team, reinforcing a positive cycle.

Celebrating Resilience Victories

Just as a football team celebrates overcoming tough opponents, HR leaders should acknowledge and celebrate victories over adversity.

Recognition and Appreciation:

- **Acknowledgment:** Acknowledge and appreciate the resilience demonstrated by individuals and the team.
- **Team Building Activities:** Organize team-building activities that celebrate collective resilience.
- **Narrative of Triumph:** Share stories of overcoming adversity to inspire and motivate the team.

Resilience in adversity enables individuals to view challenges as opportunities for growth rather than insurmountable obstacles. By embracing resilience, individuals develop the capacity to navigate setbacks with determination and resilience, turning adversity into stepping stones toward personal and professional development.

Managing the HR Season: Sustaining Performance for the Long Haul

Effectively managing the HR season requires strategic planning, consistent effort, and a focus on sustainable performance, ensuring that the HR team remains resilient and effective for the long haul.

Understanding the HR Marathon

Leading the HR function is a prolonged endeavor that requires endurance, planning, and an understanding of the long-term goals. The HR marathon encompasses ongoing responsibilities, strategic initiatives, and the continuous pursuit of organizational excellence.

Strategic Planning:

- **Long-Term Vision:** Develop a long-term vision for HR that aligns with organizational goals.
- **Roadmap Creation:** Create a roadmap outlining key milestones and initiatives for the coming years.
- **Flexibility:** Build flexibility into strategic plans to adapt to changing organizational needs.

Consistent Effort and Pace

Unlike a sprint where bursts of energy are crucial, the HR marathon demands a steady and sustainable pace.

Consistency in Execution:

- **Daily Prioritization:** Prioritize tasks and initiatives daily to maintain a consistent workflow.
- **Balanced Workload:** Ensure a balanced workload for the HR team to prevent burnout.
- **Performance Metrics:** Establish and monitor performance metrics to gauge the team's consistent effort.

Building a Resilient HR Team

Managing the HR season requires cultivating a team that is not only skilled but also resilient.

Skills Development:

- **Training and Development:** Invest in ongoing training and development to enhance team members' skills.
- **Cross-training:** Implement cross-training initiatives to ensure a versatile and adaptable team.
- **Succession Planning:** Develop succession plans to sustain leadership and expertise within the HR team.

Sustainable Performance Practices

To avoid exhaustion and maintain effectiveness, sustainable performance practices must be integrated into the HR marathon.

Wellness Programs:

- **Health and Wellness Initiatives:** Implement wellness programs to support the physical and mental well-being of the HR team.
- **Work-Life Balance:** Encourage a healthy work-life balance to prevent burnout and boost job satisfaction.
- **Regular Check-Ins:** Conduct regular check-ins to assess the team's well-being and address any concerns.

Strategic Alignment with Organizational Goals

Navigating the HR season successfully involves ensuring that HR initiatives consistently contribute to overall organizational success.

Regular Alignment Checks:

- **Strategic Reviews:** Conduct regular reviews to ensure HR initiatives align with organizational goals.
- **Adjusting Course:** Make strategic adjustments as needed to stay in sync with the organization's trajectory.

- **Continuous Improvement:** Foster a culture of continuous improvement to enhance the effectiveness of HR strategies.

Celebrating Milestones in the Marathon

Acknowledging and celebrating milestones achieved during the HR marathon keeps the team motivated and focused.

Recognition and Appreciation:

- **Milestone Celebrations:** Celebrate key achievements and milestones in the HR journey.
- **Team Recognition:** Recognize the collective efforts of the HR team in sustaining performance.
- **Motivational Boosts:** Provide motivational boosts to maintain team morale throughout the marathon.

Managing the HR season requires a combination of strategic planning and consistent effort. By approaching the HR leadership season as a marathon, leaders can ensure sustained success and long-term impact.

Strategy for HR Success: Optimizing Performance through Phases

Just as athletes use dedicated focus and training to enhance their performance, HR leaders can optimize their team's capabilities by adopting strategic focusing principles. This structured approach involves dividing the HR journey into distinct phases, each with specific focuses and objectives, ultimately leading to sustained success.

In this example, typical HR high-priority areas are highlighted.

Understanding Strategic Focus in HR

Strategic focus involves breaking down needs into defined phases, each serving a unique purpose. This approach allows you to strategically manage resources, energy, and initiatives throughout the calendar year.

Strategic Phases:

- **Planning Phase:** Initiate the year with comprehensive strategic planning, setting the tone for upcoming initiatives.

- **Execution Phase:** Implement planned initiatives, focusing on tactical execution and achieving short-term goals.

- **Reflection Phase:** Conclude the year with a reflective period, assessing achievements, lessons learned, and areas for improvement.

Planning Phase: Setting the Foundation

This phase kicks off the HR season by laying a solid foundation for upcoming initiatives.

Strategic Goal Setting:

- **Long-Term Vision:** Define a long-term vision for HR, aligning it with the organizational strategy.

- **Annual Objectives:** Set specific, measurable, and achievable objectives for the upcoming year.

- **Resource Allocation:** Allocate resources effectively, based on strengths, development opportunities, and competencies, to support planned initiatives.

Execution Phase: Tactical Implementation

Once the foundation is set, the execution phase involves putting plans into action.

Initiative Implementation:

- **Project Management:** A structured approach/methodology and tool for the HR team to create tasks, set deadlines, assign responsibilities, and manage/monitor project milestones, issues, and risks.

- **Communications and Collaboration:** Effective communication and collaboration is vital for all your initiatives. Tools like Slack,

Microsoft Teams, or Zoom provide instant messaging, video conferencing, and collaboration features that can enable your team to share files and collaborate on documents, fostering teamwork and creativity.

- **Status and Reporting:** Increase visibility to key leaders through customized status reports and visualizations. Additionally, these reports will help you stay on top of any issues or risks to your milestones.

Reflection Phase: Evaluating and Learning

The reflection phase marks the conclusion of the HR year, providing an opportunity to assess performance.

Performance Assessment:

- **Metrics Review:** Evaluate key performance metrics to gauge the success of HR initiatives.
- **Feedback Collection:** Gather feedback from HR team members and other stakeholders.
- **Lessons Learned:** Identify lessons learned and areas for improvement in the next planning cycle.

Adaptation for Ongoing Success

Strategic focus in HR is not a one-time process; it's a cycle designed for ongoing success. Adaptation is the cornerstone of ongoing success, requiring a willingness to evolve and innovate in response to changing circumstances. CHROs who prioritize adaptation empower their teams to embrace new challenges, pivot when necessary, and capitalize on emerging opportunities.

Continuous Improvement:

- **Iterative Planning:** Use insights from the reflection phase to refine and improve future plans.
- **Flexibility:** Adapt plans as needed to align with evolving organizational needs.

- **Long-Term Vision Alignment:** Ensure that each phase contributes to the realization of the long-term HR vision.

Team Engagement and Motivation

Effective communication of the purpose of each phase is essential for providing clarity on goals and fostering alignment within the team. By clearly articulating the objectives and expected outcomes of each phase, team members can better understand their roles and responsibilities, leading to improved coordination and productivity.

Communication Strategies:

- **Goal Clarity:** Communicate the goals and objectives of each phase to the team.
- **Recognition:** Acknowledge and celebrate achievements at the end of each phase.
- **Team Building:** Use each phase to strengthen team bonds and collaboration.

HR success involves planning, execution, and reflection. By adopting this strategic approach, you can optimize performance, adapt to changing needs, and create a pathway for sustained success throughout the HR season.

Celebrating Milestones: Victory Lap for HR Achievements

In the game of HR leadership, celebrating milestones isn't just a formality—it's a crucial victory lap that fuels motivation, reinforces positive behavior, and builds a culture of achievement. Just as athletes savor their victories, HR leaders should take the time to acknowledge and celebrate the significant milestones reached throughout the HR season.

Importance of Celebrating HR Milestones

Celebrating milestones goes beyond mere acknowledgment; it's a strategic practice with impacts on team morale, motivation, and the overall organizational culture.

Motivation Boost:

- **Recognition:** Acknowledging and celebrating milestones provides team members with a sense of accomplishment and recognition.
- **Positive Reinforcement:** Celebrations act as positive reinforcement, motivating the team to continue their efforts and exceed expectations.
- **Team Bonding:** Shared celebrations strengthen team bonds, fostering a sense of camaraderie and collaboration.

Strategies for Milestone Celebrations

Appropriately planning individual and team recognition is crucial for ensuring creative execution that resonates with employees. By carefully considering the preferences and achievements of each team member, HR can tailor recognition initiatives to make them more meaningful and impactful.

Tailored Recognition:

- **Individual Recognition:** Acknowledge individual achievements, showcasing the unique contributions of team members.
- **Team Celebrations:** Host team-wide events to commemorate collective achievements, emphasizing the power of collaboration.
- **Personal Touch:** Tailor celebrations to align with the preferences and personalities of team members.

Creative Celebration Ideas

Making milestones memorable involves injecting creativity into the celebration process.

Themed Events:

- **Game Day Celebration:** Transform the workplace into a game day arena, complete with themed decorations and activities.

- **Awards Ceremony:** Host an awards ceremony recognizing outstanding contributions, complete with custom trophies or certificates.

- **Team Building Activities:** Plan team-building activities that combine celebration with skill-building and collaboration.

Reflecting on Progress

Milestone celebrations not only mark significant achievements but also serve as valuable opportunities for reflection and learning. By taking the time to pause and reflect on past successes, teams can identify what went well and areas for improvement. This introspective process enables continuous growth and development, reinforcing positive behaviors and strategies while addressing any challenges encountered along the way.

Reflection Activities:

- **Roundtable Discussions:** Conduct roundtable discussions to reflect on the journey, lessons learned, and areas for improvement.

- **Goal Setting:** Use milestone celebrations to set new goals and aspirations for the upcoming phases.

- **Guest Speakers:** Invite guest speakers or industry experts to share insights and inspire the team for future milestones.

Sustaining the Celebration Culture

Embedding celebration into the DNA of the HR team requires ongoing commitment.

Regular Check-ins:

- **Frequent Celebrations:** Don't wait for major milestones; celebrate small wins and achievements regularly.

- **Feedback Loop:** Establish a feedback loop to gauge the effectiveness of celebrations and make continuous improvements.

- **Flexibility:** Be open to evolving celebration strategies to keep the process fresh and engaging.

Throughout this book, the significance of celebrating personal and organizational achievements is repeatedly emphasized as a pivotal aspect of fostering a positive and thriving work environment.

Recognizing and commemorating milestones not only acknowledges individual and collective efforts but also reinforces a sense of accomplishment and pride within the team.

Moreover, celebrating achievements serves as a strategic investment in building a strong organizational culture by promoting camaraderie, boosting morale, and reinforcing shared values.

By actively commemorating successes, organizations can cultivate a culture of appreciation, motivation, and resilience, laying the foundation for sustained growth and success.

CHAPTER 7

Analyzing Game Film for Continuous Improvement

✓ Continuous Improvement Mindset: Elevating HR through Iterative Excellence
✓ Metrics and Analytics Review: Elevating HR through Iterative Excellence
✓ Learning from Defeats: Resilience in the Face of Adversity
✓ Competitive Benchmarking: Gaining the Winning Edge
✓ The Hall of Fame Mindset: Elevating Your Game to Hall of Fame Status

Continuous Improvement Mindset: Elevating HR through Iterative Excellence

The continuous improvement mindset serves as a catalyst for HR excellence by fostering a culture of innovation, adaptability, and growth within the organization. It encourages HR professionals to proactively seek out opportunities for enhancement, refine existing processes, and optimize strategies to better meet evolving needs. By embracing continuous improvement, HR teams can drive operational efficiency, enhance employee satisfaction, and ultimately contribute to the overall success and competitiveness of the organization.

Basketball coach John Wooden once said, "It's what you learn after you know it all that counts."

As the CHRO, cultivating a continuous improvement mindset is not just a practice; it's a commitment to evolution, ensuring that your HR initiatives evolve in sync with the changing needs of the organization.

The Essence of Continuous Improvement in HR

A continuous improvement mindset is not merely a methodology but a core philosophy that underpins HR strategy, operations, and culture.

Iterative Excellence:

- **Adaptability:** Embrace change as an opportunity for growth, fostering adaptability in the face of evolving HR challenges.
- **Feedback-Driven:** Establish a feedback loop that encourages ongoing learning, improvement, and the cultivation of innovative solutions.
- **Efficiency Focus:** Streamline HR processes continually, eliminating inefficiencies and optimizing workflows for maximum impact.

Components of a Continuous Improvement Culture

A continuous improvement culture is characterized by a commitment to ongoing learning, feedback mechanisms, and iterative refinement of processes and practices. It encourages employees at all levels to actively seek opportunities for innovation, embrace change, and contribute ideas for improvement.

Learning Organization:

- **Knowledge Sharing:** Create platforms for knowledge sharing, ensuring that insights from individual experiences contribute to collective learning.
- **Training Initiatives:** Invest in ongoing training and development programs to enhance skills and stay ahead of industry trends.
- **Experimentation:** Encourage a culture of experimentation, where HR professionals feel empowered to test new strategies and approaches.

Implementing Continuous Improvement in HR Operations

Implementing continuous improvement in HR operations involves regularly reviewing existing processes, identifying areas for enhancement, and implementing changes to drive efficiency and effectiveness.

Process Optimization:

- **Root Cause Analysis:** Conduct thorough analyses to identify root causes of challenges, enabling targeted improvements rather than surface-level fixes.
- **Technology Integration:** Regularly assess and integrate innovative HR technologies that enhance efficiency and elevate the employee experience.
- **Agile Methodologies:** Apply agile methodologies to HR project management, allowing for iterative development and rapid response to changing needs.

Fostering a Culture of Innovation

Continuous improvement is inherently linked with fostering an innovative spirit within the HR team.

Innovative Thinking:

- **Idea Generation:** Cultivate an environment where team members feel encouraged to contribute ideas and innovations.

- **Creative Problem-Solving:** Empower your team to approach challenges with creativity, seeking unconventional solutions.

- **Risk-Taking:** Create a safe space for calculated risk-taking, understanding that innovation often involves stepping outside comfort zones.

Metrics and KPIs for Continuous Improvement

Measuring the impact of continuous improvement initiatives is essential for gauging success and refining strategies.

Key Performance Indicators (KPIs):

- **Efficiency Metrics:** Track improvements in HR processes, aiming for increased efficiency and reduced operational bottlenecks.

- **Employee Satisfaction:** Monitor employee satisfaction metrics to assess the impact of HR initiatives on the workforce.

- **Innovation Index:** Develop metrics that measure the frequency and success of innovative HR solutions.

In the game of HR leadership, the continuous improvement mindset is the secret play that transforms challenges into opportunities and ordinary practices into extraordinary achievements. By incorporating these practices, you can ensure that your team remains at the forefront of organizational excellence.

Metrics and Analytics Review: Playing the Data-Driven Game

In the playbook of HR leadership, metrics, and analytics serve as the game-changers, providing invaluable insights that drive informed decision-making and elevate the overall performance of the HR team. Unlocking the power of data transforms HR from a reactive player to a proactive champion in shaping the future of the organization.

The Significance of Metrics and Analytics in HR

Metrics and analytics play a crucial role in HR by providing objective insights into various aspects of workforce management, such as recruitment, retention, performance, and engagement. By leveraging data-driven decision-making, you can identify trends, patterns, and areas for improvement, allowing them to serve as the north star for more effective strategies and initiatives.

Moreover, metrics enable HR teams to track the impact of their efforts over time, measure the success of HR programs, and justify resource allocation based on quantifiable results.

Strategic Alignment:

- **Goal Alignment:** Align HR metrics with organizational goals, ensuring that every data point contributes to the broader strategic vision.
- **Proactive Decision-Making:** Leverage analytics to anticipate HR needs, enabling proactive decision-making rather than reactive responses.
- **Measuring Impact:** Demonstrate the impact of HR initiatives through quantifiable metrics that resonate with organizational objectives.

Essential HR Metrics for Performance Evaluation

Metrics and analytics play a pivotal role in evaluating the effectiveness of HR programs and initiatives by providing data-driven insights into key performance indicators and outcomes. They enable HR professionals to make informed decisions, optimize strategies, and align resources with organizational goals for continuous improvement.

Performance Metrics:

- **Employee Productivity:** Measure individual and team productivity to assess the overall efficiency of the workforce.
- **Retention Rates:** Analyze turnover rates to understand employee retention and identify areas for improvement.
- **Recruitment Effectiveness:** Evaluate the success of recruitment efforts by scrutinizing the time-to-fill, quality of hires, and diversity metrics.

Harnessing Predictive Analytics in HR

Predictive analytics is the forward-looking lens through which you can anticipate future trends and challenges.

Predictive Insights:

- **Succession Planning:** Use predictive analytics to identify high-potential employees and plan for succession strategically.
- **Talent Forecasting:** Anticipate talent needs and shortages by analyzing data trends in the external labor market.
- **Workforce Planning:** Align staffing levels with business goals by predicting future workforce requirements based on historical data.

Data-Driven Employee Experience Enhancement

Metrics and analytics provide a holistic view of the employee experience, allowing HR to make targeted improvements.

Employee Engagement Metrics:

- **Pulse Surveys:** Utilize frequent pulse surveys to measure and respond to real-time employee engagement levels.
- **Performance Feedback:** Gather data on individual and team performance, identifying areas for recognition and improvement.

- **Training Effectiveness:** Assess the impact of training programs through analytics, refining learning initiatives for maximum efficacy.

Continuous Improvement through Analytics

Continuous improvement through analytics involves leveraging data to identify trends, patterns, and areas for enhancement within HR processes and initiatives. By analyzing metrics such as employee engagement, turnover rates, and performance evaluations, HR teams can pinpoint areas of strength and weakness to refine strategies and drive positive change.

These insights enable HR professionals to make data-driven decisions, implement targeted interventions, and measure the impact of their actions over time.

Through a cycle of continuous feedback and improvement, your organization can enhance efficiency, productivity, and employee satisfaction, fostering a culture of continuous improvement and innovation.

Feedback Loops:

- **Regular Analysis:** Conduct regular reviews of HR metrics, incorporating feedback loops for continuous improvement.
- **Benchmarking:** Compare HR metrics against industry benchmarks to identify areas for improvement and innovation.
- **Data-Driven Innovations:** Use insights gained from analytics to drive innovative HR solutions and initiatives.

By embracing the power of data, HR leaders can champion a data-driven culture that propels the organization toward sustained success.

Learning from Defeats: Resilience in the Face of Adversity

Defeats are not failures but opportunities for growth. Learning from defeats cultivates resilience in individuals and teams by providing opportunities for reflection, growth, and adaptation. By analyzing setbacks, identifying root causes, and extracting valuable lessons, individuals can develop the mental toughness to overcome future challenges with confidence.

Resilience enables individuals to bounce back from failures stronger and more resilient, fostering a culture of perseverance and tenacity within the organization. Embracing defeats as learning experiences empowers your team to approach adversity with a growth mindset, turning setbacks into stepping stones toward success.

Ultimately, resilience in the face of adversity enables your team to thrive in dynamic environments, emerging stronger and more resilient from every setback.

Embracing Defeats as Learning Opportunities

Defeats and setbacks are integral parts of the HR season, offering valuable lessons that contribute to long-term success.

Post-Project Reviews:

- **Deconstructing Failures:** Conduct post-project reviews to analyze projects or initiatives that did not meet expectations.
- **Identifying Root Causes:** Explore the root causes of defeats, seeking insights that go beyond surface-level analysis.
- **Lessons for Future Projects:** Use defeat as a blueprint for improvement, applying lessons learned to enhance future initiatives.

Cultivating a Growth Mindset

Resilience in HR hinges on adopting a mindset that reframes defeats as valuable opportunities for improvement and growth. Rather than seeing setbacks as roadblocks, HR professionals who embrace resilience perceive them as essential steps in the journey toward excellence.

Mindset Shift:

- **From Fixed to Growth:** Encourage HR professionals to adopt a growth mindset, seeing defeats as opportunities to learn and evolve.
- **Celebrating Effort:** Recognize and celebrate the effort put forth by the HR team, emphasizing the importance of continuous improvement.

Creating a Supportive Environment

Learning from defeat necessitates a collaborative and supportive workplace culture where individuals feel empowered to share their experiences openly. By fostering an environment where team members can discuss setbacks without fear of judgment, organizations can extract valuable lessons and collectively strive for improvement.

Team Reflection Sessions:

- **Open Dialogue:** Foster an environment where team members can openly discuss defeats without fear of blame.
- **Shared Responsibility:** Emphasize that defeats are shared responsibilities and not individual failures.
- **Constructive Feedback:** Provide constructive feedback to guide improvement, focusing on actionable insights.

Implementing Corrective Actions

Resilience extends beyond bouncing back from setbacks; it entails leveraging lessons learned to implement strategic changes. This proactive approach involves analyzing the root causes of challenges and devising innovative solutions to prevent similar issues in the future.

By embracing a culture of continuous improvement, organizations can adapt to evolving circumstances and enhance their resilience over time.

Strategic Adjustments:

- **Adapting Strategies:** Adjust HR strategies based on the insights gained from defeats, ensuring a more informed approach.
- **Skill Enhancement:** Identify skill gaps or areas for improvement and invest in training and development.
- **Iterative Approach:** Embrace an iterative approach, allowing the HR team to evolve and refine its methods continuously.

Measuring Resilience Metrics

Resilience amidst defeat can be quantified by metrics reflecting the team's capacity to adapt and enhance performance. These metrics serve as indicators of the team's ability to learn from setbacks and implement effective strategies for future success.

Resilience Metrics:

- **Turnaround Time:** Measure the time it takes for the team to rebound from setbacks and implement corrective actions.
- **Adaptability Index:** Assess the team's adaptability to changing circumstances and its ability to learn from defeats.
- **Employee Satisfaction:** Monitor employee satisfaction during challenging times, gauging the team's resilience.

In the playbook of HR leadership, defeats are not the end of the game, but a gametime reset. By learning from defeat, HR teams cultivate a resilient spirit that not only survives challenges but thrives on them, emerging stronger, more adaptive, and ready for the next strategic play.

Competitive Benchmarking: Gaining the Winning Edge

Understanding where you stand in comparison to competitors is the key to securing the winning edge. Competitive benchmarking is the playbook that empowers CHROs to not only keep pace with industry standards but also to surpass them strategically.

Strategic Positioning Through Benchmarking

To stay ahead, it's crucial to have a comprehensive grasp of how your HR practices stack up against industry benchmarks and competitors. This insight enables you to identify areas of strength and weakness, allowing for strategic adjustments to maintain a competitive edge.

Identifying Key Performance Indicators (KPIs):

- **Strategic Alignment:** Pinpoint the HR areas that are critical for strategic alignment with organizational goals.

- **Employee Engagement:** Measure employee engagement metrics to gauge the effectiveness of HR initiatives.

- **Talent Acquisition and Retention:** Assess the efficiency of talent acquisition and retention strategies in comparison to competitors.

Competitor Analysis for Informed Decision-Making

Gaining insights into your competitors' HR practices is akin to studying an opponent's playbook – it informs your strategy and reveals opportunities for improvement. By understanding how other organizations approach talent management, recruitment, and employee engagement, you can identify areas where you excel and areas where you can gain a competitive advantage. This knowledge empowers you to refine your HR strategies, stay innovative, and maintain relevance in the market.

SWOT Analysis:

- **Strengths and Weaknesses:** Identify competitors' strengths and weaknesses in HR management, learning from their successes and avoiding their pitfalls.
- **Opportunities and Threats:** Analyze the opportunities and threats in the HR landscape, adapting strategies to maximize opportunities and mitigate threats.

Adapting Best Practices for HR Excellence

Competitive benchmarking is not about imitation but about adapting best practices to suit your organization's unique needs.

Best Practice Integration:

- **Adopting Innovative Approaches:** Incorporate innovative HR approaches employed by leading competitors.
- **Customization for Your Organization:** Tailor best practices to align with your organization's culture, values, and strategic goals.

Continuous Monitoring and Adjustment

Competitive benchmarking is an ongoing process that requires continuous monitoring to ensure sustained excellence.

Regular Performance Reviews:

- **Scheduled Assessments:** Establish regular intervals for benchmarking assessments to track changes and improvements.
- **Course Correction:** Use benchmarking results as a compass for strategic course corrections, ensuring alignment with industry trends.

Building a Culture of Excellence

Competitive benchmarking not only enhances HR performance but also contributes to building a culture of continuous improvement and excellence. By regularly assessing how your HR practices stack up against industry standards and competitors, you can identify areas for improvement and innovation.

This process fosters a mindset of learning and adaptation within the HR team, encouraging them to seek out best practices and implement changes proactively. Additionally, benchmarking allows you and your team to track progress over time, set realistic goals, and measure success against industry benchmarks.

Ultimately, it enables organizations to stay agile, responsive, and competitive in attracting, retaining, and developing top talent.

Competitive benchmarking is the secret weapon that propels your team to the forefront. By understanding the competitive landscape, you can strategically position your organizations for success, setting the stage for sustained excellence.

The Hall of Fame Mindset: Elevating Your Game to Hall of Fame Status

Adopting the Hall of Fame mindset transforms CHROs into legends. As mentioned in Chapter 1, adopting this mindset embodies a culture of recognition and appreciation for the unique contributions of every team member, regardless of their role or position within the organization.

It emphasizes the importance of acknowledging and valuing individual strengths, skills, and perspectives, recognizing that leveraging these diverse talents is instrumental in driving organizational success.

By fostering an inclusive environment where each member feels empowered to contribute their best, you can harness the collective power of the team to achieve shared goals and propel the organization forward.

Setting the Stage for the Hall of Fame

The Hall of Fame mindset is an evolution beyond merely being the Most Valuable Player– it's about becoming a Master of Vision and Performance.

Visionary Leadership Reinvented:

- **Strategic Vision Integration:** Align your leadership vision with the organization's strategic goals, creating a roadmap for excellence.
- **Continuous Innovation:** Embrace a mindset of consistent innovation, seeking solutions to old challenges.

Championing Change and Adaptability

The Hall of Fame mindset champions adaptability and change as the cornerstones of success. It recognizes that embracing change and being adaptable are crucial traits for thriving in today's dynamic business environment.

Agile Decision-Making:

- **Swift Adaptation:** Respond to shifts in the HR landscape with agility, making informed decisions promptly.
- **Change Leadership:** Act as a change champion, inspiring the HR team to navigate transitions seamlessly.

Strategic Talent Management Mastery

Being an HR Hall of Famer involves not just managing talent but mastering the art of strategically shaping the workforce. It requires the ability to align human capital with organizational goals, anticipate future talent needs, and develop initiatives to attract, retain, and develop top talent.

CHROs in this league understand the significance of building diverse and inclusive teams that drive innovation and foster a culture of belonging. They leverage data-driven insights to make informed decisions and continuously refine HR strategies to meet evolving business needs.

Holistic Talent Development:

- **Identifying High-Potentials:** Spot high-potential individuals and nurture their growth within the organization.
- **Succession Planning:** Develop robust succession plans, ensuring a pipeline of future leaders.

Data-Driven Decision Excellence

The Hall of Fame mindset leverages the power of data for precision decision-making, elevating HR strategies to new heights. By harnessing data analytics, HR leaders gain valuable insights into workforce trends, employee engagement, and performance metrics, enabling them to make informed decisions that drive organizational success. This data-driven approach empowers HR teams to optimize talent management practices, identify areas for improvement, and implement targeted initiatives to support the company's strategic objectives.

Metrics Mastery:

- **Advanced Analytics:** Harness advanced analytics to derive deep insights into HR performance.
- **Predictive Modeling:** Use predictive modeling to anticipate HR trends and make proactive decisions.

Empowering and Inspiring Teams

Beyond individual excellence, the Hall of Famer focuses on empowering and inspiring HR teams for collective success. By fostering a culture of collaboration and shared purpose, HR leaders cultivate an environment where each team member's strengths are leveraged to achieve common goals. This collective approach not only enhances team performance but also fosters innovation and drives organizational growth.

Team Cohesion Enhancement:

- **Leadership Development:** Invest in leadership development programs, cultivating a culture of growth and empowerment.
- **Inclusive Leadership:** Foster an inclusive leadership approach that values diverse perspectives and contributions.

Legacy Building Through Mentorship

An HR Hall of Fame legacy extends beyond accomplishments to the mentorship and development of future leaders. These seasoned professionals understand that their impact is measured not only by their achievements but also by the success of those they nurture and guide.

By sharing their knowledge, experiences, and insights, they cultivate a new generation of HR talent equipped to navigate the challenges of tomorrow. Through mentorship programs, leadership workshops, and continuous learning initiatives, they invest in the growth and advancement of aspiring HR professionals.

Their commitment to building a pipeline of capable leaders ensures the sustainability and longevity of HR excellence in organizations.

Mentorship Programs:

- **Strategic Guidance:** Provide strategic guidance to emerging HR professionals, contributing to their career growth.
- **Knowledge Transfer:** Share insights and experiences to build a legacy of excellence within the HR function.

The Hall of Fame is the pinnacle of HR leadership, propelling CHROs to legendary status. By embracing visionary leadership, and championing change, HR leaders can leave a memorable mark on the organization and the profession.

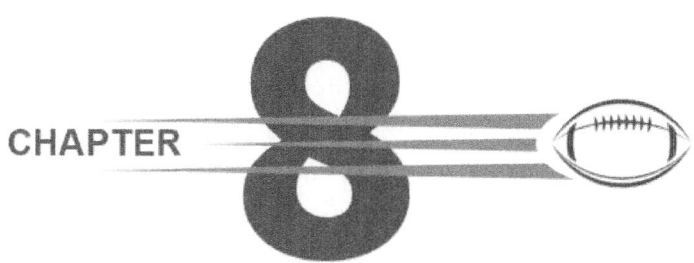

CHAPTER 8

Strategic Planning for the Upcoming Season

- ✓ Reflecting on the Current Season: Evaluating Wins, Losses, and Lessons
- ✓ Defining Long-term Objectives: Charting a Course for HR Success
- ✓ Tactical Adjustments for Success: Navigating the HR Playbook
- ✓ Resource Allocation Strategies: Maximizing HR Impact
- ✓ Meet Your Referee: HR Compliance
- ✓ The 3-Month CHRO Strategic Plan: A Winning Playbook

Reflecting on the Current Season: Evaluating Wins, Losses, and Lessons

As the CHRO, leading the HR team is a season-long performance, complete with victories, setbacks, and invaluable lessons.

Inspired by the words of Super Bowl-winning football coach Bill Parcells, who said, "You are what your record says you are," this chapter challenges you to take an inward look at the achievements and shortcomings of your HR strategies.

As we dissect the game's plays, we find both successes and failures, and we extract insights that will guide your future leadership moves. Now, let's review the HR season's scorecard, making the most of each victory and every setback to prepare for future successes that will be even more strategic and powerful.

1. Performance Evaluation

Assessing Wins:

- Celebrating Achievements: Recognize and celebrate HR wins, acknowledging successful projects, talent acquisitions, and strategic milestones.
- Identifying Key Contributors: Highlight the contributions of individuals and teams who played pivotal roles in HR successes.

Analyzing Losses:

- Root Cause Analysis: Dive deep into areas where HR initiatives faced challenges, identifying root causes for setbacks.
- Learning Opportunities: View losses not as failures but as opportunities for growth and improvement.

2. Stakeholder Feedback Sessions

Engaging with Key Stakeholders:

- Executive Leadership: Seek feedback from executive leadership on HR's impact on organizational goals and areas for improvement.
- Departmental Heads: Collaborate with departmental heads to understand specific HR needs within various teams.

Employee Surveys:

- Gauging Employee Satisfaction: Conduct surveys to gauge employee satisfaction with HR services and initiatives.
- Identifying Pain Points: Uncover pain points and concerns, ensuring HR addresses employee needs effectively.

3. Metrics and KPIs Review

Analyzing HR Metrics:

- Key Performance Indicators (KPIs): Scrutinize HR metrics and KPIs to measure the effectiveness of various initiatives.
- Identifying Trends: Spot trends in workforce engagement, retention, and other critical areas.

4. Learning from Challenges

Turning Challenges into Opportunities:

- Post-Mortem Analysis: Conduct post-mortem analyses on challenges faced by HR during the season.
- Implementing Corrective Measures: Take corrective measures based on lessons learned to enhance future performance.

5. Strategizing for the Next Season

Setting Strategic Goals:

- Long-Term Vision: Align HR strategies with the organization's long-term vision and goals.
- Continuous Improvement: Develop strategies for continuous improvement, ensuring HR remains agile and adaptable.

Tactical Adjustments:

- Implementing Feedback: Integrate stakeholder feedback and employee insights into tactical adjustments for the upcoming season.
- Fine-tuning processes: Refine HR processes and workflows based on lessons learned and emerging industry trends.

Reflecting on the current season is not just about looking back – it's about gaining insights that fuel a stronger, more strategic HR leadership in the seasons ahead. By assessing wins, learning from losses, engaging with stakeholders, reviewing metrics, and strategizing for the future, you can elevate your game and lead HR to unprecedented success.

Defining Long-Term Objectives: Charting a Course for HR Success

Defining long-term objectives is paramount for charting a course toward HR success. These objectives serve as guiding stars, providing clarity and direction amidst the complexities of the HR landscape. By articulating clear and measurable goals, you can rally your team around a shared vision and inspire commitment to achieving strategic milestones. Long-term objectives also enable the HR function to align initiatives with broader organizational priorities, ensuring coherence and synergy across the business. Through thoughtful planning and foresight, you and your team can anticipate future challenges and proactively develop solutions to drive sustainable growth and competitive advantage. By regularly reviewing and adjusting long-term objectives, HR remains agile and responsive to evolving needs, positioning the organization for success in the ever-changing business environment.

1. Visionary HR Leadership

Crafting a Vision:

- **Envisioning the Future:** Define a compelling and aspirational vision for the HR function, aligning it with the overall organizational vision.

- **Inspiring Stakeholders:** Communicate the vision in a way that inspires and rallies HR professionals and key stakeholders.

Strategic Alignment:

- **Linking to Organizational Goals:** Ensure that long-term HR objectives are intricately linked to the broader strategic goals of the organization.

- **Contributing to Success:** Clarify how HR success contributes directly to the overall success of the company.

2. Talent Management Excellence

Building a Robust Talent Pipeline:

- **Identifying Critical Roles:** Identify key roles critical for organizational success and develop a strategy for talent management.

- **Succession Planning:** Implement robust succession planning to ensure a steady pipeline of qualified internal candidates.

Employee Development Initiatives:

- **Continuous Learning Culture:** Foster a culture of continuous learning, providing employees with opportunities for skill development.

- **Leadership Development Programs:** Institute programs to groom future HR leaders from within the organization.

3. Diversity, Equity, and Inclusion (DEI) Integration

Embedding DEI Principles:

- **Inclusive Workforce:** Set objectives for creating a diverse and inclusive workforce that reflects varied perspectives.

- **Equity in Opportunities:** Ensure equal opportunities for career growth, irrespective of background or demographics.

Measuring DEI Progress:

- **Establishing Metrics:** Define metrics to track progress in diversity, equity, and inclusion initiatives.

- **Adapting Strategies:** Continuously adapt strategies to address evolving challenges and opportunities in DEI.

4. Technological Advancements

HR Technology Roadmap:

- **Assessing Current Tech Landscape:** Evaluate the existing HR technology stack, identifying areas for enhancement and optimization.

- **Investment Strategies:** Define a roadmap for adopting new technologies that enhance HR efficiency and effectiveness.

Automation and Innovation:

- **Process Automation:** Set objectives for automating routine HR processes to streamline operations.

- **Innovative Solutions:** Encourage a culture of innovation, fostering the adoption of cutting-edge HR solutions.

5. Workplace Culture Transformation

Cultural Objectives:

- **Defining Desired Culture:** Clearly articulate the desired workplace culture aligned with organizational values.

- **Employee Well-Being:** Prioritize employee well-being as a cornerstone of the organizational culture.

Communication Strategies:

- **Transparent Communication:** Establish objectives for transparent and effective communication within the organization.

- **Feedback Mechanisms:** Implement feedback mechanisms to gauge employee sentiment and make culture-related adjustments.

Defining long-term objectives in HR leadership is not merely about setting goals; it's about envisioning a future where HR is a strategic driver of organizational success. By aligning with the organization's vision, focusing on talent management, integrating DEI principles, leveraging technology, and transforming workplace culture, CHROs can set a course for enduring success in the ever-evolving business landscape.

Tactical Adjustments for Success: Navigating the HR Playbook

In Human Resources stadium, the ability to make tactical adjustments is the secret weapon for success. It's about staying agile, adapting to changing conditions, and ensuring that HR strategies are finely tuned for optimal performance.

1. Agile HR Strategies

Responsive Talent Acquisition:

- **Flexibility in Recruitment:** Develop strategies for adapting to changing hiring needs, ensuring a responsive and agile talent acquisition process.

- **Embracing Remote Work:** Adjust recruitment strategies to accommodate and optimize remote work opportunities.

Adaptable Training Programs:

- **Continuous Learning Modules:** Design training programs that can be easily adapted to address emerging skill requirements.

- **Virtual Training Platforms:** Invest in virtual training platforms to facilitate ongoing learning in a digital landscape.

2. Dynamic Employee Engagement

Real-time Feedback Mechanisms:

- **Pulse Surveys:** Implement real-time feedback mechanisms, such as pulse surveys, to gauge employee sentiment and make immediate adjustments.

- **Agile Recognition Programs:** Develop agile employee recognition programs that can be adjusted based on evolving performance criteria.

Innovative Communication Strategies:

- **Interactive Communication Platforms:** Utilize interactive communication platforms to foster engagement and adapt communication strategies based on employee preferences.

- **Responsive Internal Messaging:** Ensure internal messaging is responsive to current events and organizational developments.

3. Tech Integration for Efficiency

HRIS Optimization:

- **Regular System Audits:** Conduct regular audits of HRIS systems to identify areas for optimization and efficiency improvements.

- **Integration of New Technologies:** Explore and integrate emerging technologies that enhance HR processes and streamline workflows.

- **Data-Driven Decision-Making:**

  - **Metrics Review:** Establish a routine for reviewing HR metrics and analytics, allowing for data-driven decision-making and adjustments.

  - **Predictive Analytics Integration:** Invest in predictive analytics tools to anticipate HR needs and proactively make tactical adjustments.

4. Crisis Management Agility

Preparedness Protocols:

- **Crisis Response Plans:** Develop and refine crisis response plans that can be activated swiftly in unforeseen circumstances.

- **Communication Protocols:** Establish clear communication protocols for disseminating information during a crisis.

Adaptive Leadership:

- **Rapid Decision-Making:** Foster a culture of rapid decision-making during crises, allowing for quick adjustments to HR strategies.

- **Team Mobilization:** Ensure HR teams are mobilized and ready to respond effectively in crisis situations.

5. Continuous Improvement Mindset

Feedback-Driven Optimization:

- **Continuous Feedback Loops:** Establish continuous feedback loops with HR teams to identify areas for improvement.

- **Iterative Process Enhancement:** Implement an iterative approach to process enhancement, making ongoing adjustments based on feedback.

Agile Project Management:

- **Scrum Methodology:** Embrace agile project management methodologies like Scrum to enhance project flexibility and adaptability.

- **Rapid Iterations:** Plan for rapid iterations in HR projects, allowing for quick adjustments as needed.

Tactical adjustments in HR leadership are the linchpin of success, ensuring that strategies remain effective in the face of constant change. By fostering agility in talent acquisition, adapting engagement strategies, integrating technology efficiently, preparing for crises, and maintaining a continuous improvement mindset, you and your team can navigate the dynamic HR playbook with finesse, achieving sustained success in an ever-evolving business landscape.

Resource Allocation Strategies: Maximizing HR Impact

In the game of HR, resource allocation is the strategic lever that determines where to invest for maximum impact. It's about aligning human, financial, and technological resources to achieve organizational goals efficiently.

1. Strategic Workforce Planning:

Skill Mapping and Alignment:

- **Strategic Skill Mapping:** Conduct comprehensive skill mapping to identify critical skills required for organizational success.

- **Alignment with Organizational Goals:** Align workforce planning with the organization's long-term objectives, ensuring resources are directed toward priority areas.

Succession Planning:

- **Identifying Key Roles:** Identify key roles and competencies critical to the organization's success and develop succession plans for these positions.

- **Cross-Training Initiatives:** Implement cross-training initiatives to build a versatile workforce and mitigate risks associated with key personnel transitions.

2. Technology Investment Prioritization:

HR Tech Landscape Assessment:

- **Evaluate Current Systems:** Assess the effectiveness of existing HR technology, identifying areas for improvement.

- **Emerging Technologies Exploration:** Explore emerging technologies to determine their potential impact on HR processes and employee experience.

Strategic Automation:

- **Identify Repetitive Tasks:** Identify routine HR tasks suitable for automation to free up human resources for more strategic initiatives.

- **Employee Self-Service Platforms:** Invest in employee self-service platforms to streamline HR processes and enhance employee experience.

3. Training and Development Optimization:

Critical Skill Development:

- **Identify Critical Skills:** Determine critical skills necessary for organizational growth and development.

- **Prioritize Training Programs:** Prioritize training programs that address identified skill gaps and align with strategic objectives.

Leadership Development Initiatives:

- **Identify Future Leaders:** Identify potential leaders within the organization and invest in targeted development programs.

- **Align with Organizational Goals:** Ensure leadership development initiatives align with the organization's long-term goals and culture.

4. Flexible Budgeting Approaches:

Zero-Based Budgeting:

- **Start from Scratch:** Implement zero-based budgeting to reassess budgetary needs from the ground up.

- **Prioritize High-Impact Areas:** Prioritize areas with the highest impact on HR goals and organizational success.

Contingency Planning:

- **Emergency Fund Allocation:** Allocate a portion of the budget to an emergency fund for unforeseen HR challenges.

- **Scenario Planning:** Develop scenarios for resource allocation based on different organizational and market conditions.

5. External Partnerships and Collaborations:

Strategic Vendor Relationships:

- **Evaluate Vendor Performance:** Regularly evaluate the performance of external HR service providers and adjust partnerships accordingly.

- **Negotiation for Value:** Negotiate contracts to ensure maximum value for services rendered.

6. Collaboration with Industry Experts:

- **Networking and Collaboration:** Foster collaboration with industry experts and HR thought leaders to gain insights and best practices.

- **Participation in Forums and Conferences:** Attend relevant forums and conferences to stay updated on HR trends and potential partnerships.

Effective resource allocation is the linchpin of HR impact. By strategically planning workforce needs, prioritizing technology investments, optimizing training and development, adopting flexible budgeting approaches, and forging valuable external partnerships, you can ensure that resources are allocated where they matter most, driving organizational success in the ever-evolving business arena.

Meet Your Referee: HR Compliance

In Human Resources stadium, compliance acts as the officials and referees that govern the rules of the football game. Just as they maintain order on the field and enforce the rules, HR compliance serves as the foundation that holds the company together, ensuring that you're operating within the bounds of regulations and avoiding penalties.

While the referees uphold the integrity of the football game, HR compliance safeguards your organization's integrity and secures its long-term success.

The following strategies underscore the significance of HR compliance in keeping your team in the game and propelling it toward sustainable success.

Legal Obligations and Risk Mitigation:

HR compliance ensures that organizations adhere to federal, state, and local laws and regulations governing employment practices. From anti-discrimination laws to wage and hour regulations, compliance mitigates legal risks, shielding the organization from costly fines, lawsuits, and reputational damage.

1. **Understanding Legal Frameworks:**
   Compliance begins with understanding the legal frameworks governing employment practices. The HR team must stay abreast of evolving laws and regulations, ensuring that policies and procedures align with current legal standards. Whether it's ensuring pay equity, providing reasonable accommodations, or maintaining accurate recordkeeping, adherence to legal obligations is non-negotiable.

2. **Mitigating Legal Risks:**
   Failure to comply with employment laws can result in horrible consequences. Penalties for non-compliance range from hefty

fines to civil lawsuits, damaging both finances and the company's reputation.

Moreover, the intangible costs of litigation—such as diminished employee morale and public scrutiny—can be equally devastating. HR compliance acts as a shield against legal pitfalls, minimizing risks and safeguarding the organization's interests.

3. Navigating Regulatory Complexity:
The landscape of employment law is complex, posing challenges for organizations of all sizes and industries.

From overlapping regulations to jurisdictional nuances, navigating the regulatory maze requires specific attention and expertise.

The HR team plays a pivotal role in interpreting and implementing legal requirements, ensuring that the organization remains in full compliance.

4. Fostering a Culture of Compliance:
HR compliance is not solely the responsibility of the HR department; it's a collective effort that permeates every level of the organization.

Cultivating a culture of compliance requires proactive communication, comprehensive training, and robust enforcement mechanisms. By instilling a shared commitment to ethical conduct and legal adherence, organizations can mitigate risks and fortify their foundations of integrity.

Employee Protection and Fair Treatment: Upholding HR compliance fosters an environment of fairness and equity. Policies and procedures safeguard employee rights, including protections against discrimination, harassment, and retaliation. Compliance ensures that employees are treated ethically and respectfully, fostering a culture of trust and inclusivity.

1. Promoting Equal Opportunities:

HR compliance ensures that every individual, regardless of race, gender, age, sexual orientation, disability, or any other characteristic, has equal access to employment opportunities.

Through comprehensive anti-discrimination policies and unbiased recruitment and selection processes, your company should strive to create a level playing field where merit and qualifications reign supreme.

2. Preventing Harassment and Hostile Work Environments:

Workplaces free from harassment and hostility are essential for employee well-being and productivity. HR compliance mandates policies and procedures to prevent and address harassment in all forms, including sexual harassment, bullying, and intimidation.

By fostering a culture of respect and zero tolerance for inappropriate behavior, your company can cultivate an environment where every employee feels safe and valued.

3. Ensuring Fair Compensation and Benefits:

Equitable compensation and benefits are cornerstones of fair treatment in the workplace. HR compliance involves conducting regular audits to ensure pay equity across gender, race, and other protected characteristics.

Additionally, compliance ensures that employees receive fair and competitive benefits packages, including healthcare, retirement plans, and other perks, fostering employee satisfaction and retention.

4. Providing Reasonable Accommodations:

Employees with disabilities are entitled to reasonab. accommodations to perform their job duties effectively.

HR compliance mandates proactive efforts to identify and implement accommodations that enable individuals with disabilities to participate fully in the workplace.

5. Empowering Employees to Speak Up:

Effective compliance requires mechanisms for employees to report violations of policies and seek recourse without fear of retaliation. HR plays a critical role in creating channels for open communication and ensuring confidentiality for whistleblowers.

Data Privacy and Security: In an era of increasing digitalization, protecting sensitive employee data is paramount. HR compliance encompasses adherence to data privacy laws.

1. Adhering to Data Privacy Laws:

HR compliance entails strict adherence to data privacy laws and regulations, such as the General Data Protection Regulation (GDPR) in the European Union and the Health Insurance Portability and Accountability Act (HIPAA) in the United States.

These regulations govern the collection, processing, storage, and sharing of personal information, imposing obligations to protect employee privacy rights.

2. Securing Sensitive Employee Information:

Employee data, including personal, financial, and health information, is an asset that must be protected from unauthorized access, disclosure, or misuse.

liance mandates security measures, such as
., access controls, and regular audits, to safeguard
ve data from internal and external threats.

3. Ensuring Confidentiality and Trust:
Employees entrust HR with sensitive information, expecting confidentiality and discretion in handling their personal data.

Compliance requires clear policies and procedures for data handling, including guidelines for accessing, storing, and disposing of employee information.

4. Managing Data Breach Preparedness:
Despite best efforts, data breaches can occur, posing risks to employee privacy and organizational reputation. HR compliance involves proactive planning and response strategies to mitigate the impact of data breaches.

This includes developing incident response plans, conducting regular training and drills, and collaborating with IT and legal teams to swiftly address breaches.

5. Embracing Ethical Data Practices:
Beyond legal mandates, HR compliance encompasses ethical principles for data management.

Organizations must be transparent about their data practices, obtaining informed consent from employees before collecting or processing their personal information.

Workplace Safety and Health: The well-being of employees is a fundamental priority. By implementing safety protocols, training initiatives, and emergency preparedness plans, compliance minimizes workplace hazards and promotes employee welfare.

1. Compliance with Occupational Safety and Health Administration (OSHA) Regulations:

HR compliance begins with adherence to OSHA regulatio which set forth standards and guidelines for workplace safet and health. These regulations cover a wide range of topics, including hazard communication, personal protective equipment (PPE), ergonomics, and emergency preparedness. Compliance involves conducting regular inspections, identifying hazards, and implementing corrective actions to mitigate risks and ensure compliance with OSHA standards.

2. Creating a Culture of Safety:

HR plays a pivotal role in cultivating a culture of safety within the organization. This involves fostering awareness, promoting safety training and education, and encouraging proactive hazard reporting. By empowering employees to prioritize safety and take ownership of their well-being, organizations create an environment where safety becomes a shared responsibility and a core value.

3. Implementing Safety Protocols and Procedures:

HR compliance entails developing and implementing safety protocols and procedures to prevent workplace accidents and injuries. This includes establishing clear guidelines for equipment use, handling hazardous materials, and responding to emergencies.

5. Supporting Employee Health and Wellness:

Employee health and wellness are integral components of workplace safety. HR compliance includes initiatives to support physical and mental well-being, such as wellness programs, employee assistance programs (EAPs), and access to healthcare resources.

6. Addressing Workplace Hazards and Risks:

Identifying and addressing workplace hazards is essential for maintaining a safe and healthy work environment. HR

4. Whistleblower Protection and Reporting Mechanisms:

Encouraging employees to speak up against ethical violations is essential for maintaining organizational integrity.

HR compliance involves implementing whistleblower protection policies and establishing confidential reporting mechanisms for employees to report unethical behavior or misconduct.

In Human Resources stadium, compliance is not merely a sideline concern but an integral part of your game plan for success. Just as every football team relies on the officials to ensure fair play and uphold the rules, your organization depends on HR compliance to maintain integrity and sustainability.

As a well-executed game plan can lead to victory on the football field, a comprehensive approach to HR compliance can position your company for continued success and championship seasons for years to come.

The 3-Month CHRO Strategic Plan: A Winning Playbook

This is the locker room, and here is your locker.

As you step into the role of CHRO, you should be thrilled to tackle the journey of collaboration, innovation, and impactful transformation. Your approach should be anchored in a human-centric focus, weaving together the challenges of people management with the broader fabric of organizational success.

Understanding the Landscape:

In the game's first quarter, you should intend to dedicate considerable time to immerse yourself in the organizational culture and dynamics. This begins with a series of one-on-one meetings with you and other key executives. These sessions are not just about understanding roles and responsibilities; they're a gateway to comprehending the heartbeat of your new company. By further defining your vision, aspirations, and strategic objectives, you should aim to align HR strategies seamlessly with the broader canvas of company goals.

Assessing Pain Points for Strategic Remediation:

Identifying and addressing pain points is critical for fostering a resilient and engaged workforce. You should plan to conduct comprehensive assessments to discern areas that might be impeding both individual and collective success. These evaluations will involve not just data analysis but also conversations with employees across different levels. Your assessment of the intricacies of daily challenges and recognitions is vital for crafting tailored HR interventions.

Consistent Progress Reviews:

Progressing into the 2nd and 3rd quarter of the game is not a destination. Regular check-ins will be instrumental in ensuring that your HR strategies align with the ever-evolving needs of your company. You should incorporate a bi-weekly cadence of progress reviews with key executives, providing a platform to discuss achievements, challenges, and potential adjustments. This agile approach ensures that you'll remain adaptive to the dynamic nature of your industry and workforce.

People-Centric Initiatives:

A central tenet of your strategy should be to initiate people-centric initiatives that resonate with the culture of the company. This involves developing targeted employee engagement programs, refining talent acquisition strategies, and fortifying your commitment to diversity, equity, and inclusion. These initiatives should be shaped not just by leveraging industry best practices but also by the unique spirit and aspirations of your workforce.

Building a Collaborative HR Ecosystem:

To amplify your impact, foster a collaborative environment. This involves forging strong partnerships with department heads, team leaders, and individual contributors. By embedding HR as a strategic partner in every facet of the organization, you can leverage the collective intelligence and creativity that resides within the company.

Innovative Training and Development:

As the 4th quarter of the game begins, consider the investment of your people's growth as part of the investment of the future for your company. Plan to evaluate and potentially revitalize your training and development programs, ensuring they are not only aligned with organizational goals but also reflective of emerging industry trends. This includes harnessing digital platforms for continuous learning and creating pathways for leadership development.

Elevating HR Metrics:

As the game has concluded and you begin to review the game film, metrics are not just indicators; they are storytellers. Commit to assessing, refining, and elevating your HR metrics, ensuring they encapsulate the real essence of your workforce's health and productivity. From employee satisfaction scores to talent retention rates, these metrics will serve as your compass, guiding your strategic decisions.

Final Thoughts:

In your first 3 months, the focus should be on providing value and laying the foundation for an HR function that is not just functional, but inspirational. The success of your company is intertwined with the growth, satisfaction, and innovation of its people. In collaboration with your team and peers, you can shape an HR narrative that not only meets the needs of today but also propels the company into a future of sustained success.

Executing Your Playbook

First Week – Establishing Visionary Leadership and Assessing the Playing Field

Day 1: Introduction and Welcome:

- Meet with key executives, including the CEO, to understand their perspectives, expectations, and strategic goals.

  - Understand the key revenue and expense drivers, as well as competitive dynamics.

  - Assess current budgeting and forecasting processes and timelines.

- Accomplish your onboarding and get the small stuff out of the way.

  - Get familiar with your new laptop and configure as needed.

  - Mobile phone set-up with email (and application access).

  - Outlook and mobile phone email signatures created and set.

  - Building access/key fob, parking pass, etc.

  - Benefits enrollment and necessary instructions, etc.

- Additionally, update your LinkedIn profile and send a post announcing your new position.

Day 2-3: Stakeholder Meetings:

- Conduct one-on-one sessions with department heads, team leaders, and HR team members to build relationships and gain insights into current HR processes.

- ☐ Review organizational charts, office/personnel locations, roles, responsibilities, and spans of control.

- ☐ Assess the current state reporting structure.

- ☐ Collaborate with the communications team to craft an organizational announcement about assuming the role of CHRO.

Day 4-5: Technology Familiarization:

- ☐ Familiarize yourself with the existing technologies, including existing HRIS, Payroll, and Talent Management.

- ☐ Ensure that you have access to all necessary applications, file drives, and pertinent files, and understand data flow, reporting capabilities, and potential areas for improvement.

First Month – Offensive Strategy Kickoff and Defensive Resilience Tactics

Week 2-3: Organizational Deep Dive:

- ☐ Conduct comprehensive interviews with employees across various levels to understand their experiences, challenges, and aspirations.

  - ☐ Begin identifying pain points and areas for improvement.

- ☐ Review and understand key HR policies and procedures.

- ☐ Review any past employee engagement surveys, pulse surveys, and results.

- ☐ Evaluate recruiting & staffing to understand how the company builds its brand to attract top talent.

- ☐ Review onboarding and orientation to assess whether the organization provides a consistent experience for new hires.

- [ ] Review and understand any internal total rewards philosophies in place.

- [ ] Review existing compensation strategies (base salary, short- & long-term incentives, as well as any legal and summary plan documents.

- [ ] Review any employment agreements in place, including any change-in-control or severance agreements.

- [ ] Understand the Learning & Development strategy, processes, and tools, to assess effectiveness in providing employees with rich experiences.

- [ ] Understand the current EEO and FMLA program, documentation and remediation of exceptions, and reporting of results.

- [ ] Review approach to HR Records retention to conform with State, EEO AAP, OSHA, and State/Federal Tax reporting.

- [ ] Familiarize yourself with payroll processes, controls, and cycles, employee type by pay frequency, legal entities, time capture and expense reporting processes, and any unique, customized processes and systems.

- [ ] Review current benefit programs, service agreements for all providers, plan documents, and timing for renewals.

Week 4: Initial Progress Review:

- [ ] Schedule a meeting with the CEO for an initial progress review. Share insights gathered during the first month and discuss findings of potential quick wins and strategic adjustments.

- [ ] Continue with any unresolved weeks 2 and 3 activities.

- [ ] Create a high-level plan to support month 2 and 3 activities.

Second Month – Special Teams Preparation

Week 5: Employee Engagement Survey:

☐ Collaborate with the HR team to design an employee engagement survey tailored to the unique culture of the company.

☐ Schedule and facilitate a second round of one-on-one sessions with department heads, team leaders, and HR team members to foster relationships and gain additional insights into strengths and development opportunities.

Week 6-7: Talent Management Strategy Review:

☐ Analyze current talent management strategies.

  ☐ Evaluate the effectiveness of recruitment strategies, including sourcing channels, candidate selection methods, and time-to-fill metrics.

  ☐ Assess the alignment of training and development initiatives with organizational goals and individual career paths.

  ☐ Review the effectiveness of performance appraisal processes, goal-setting methodologies, and feedback mechanisms.

  ☐ Evaluate success plans and the depth and breadth of the talent pipeline for key roles with the company.

Week 8: Bi-Weekly Progress Review:

☐ Conduct a bi-weekly progress review with the CEO. Discuss progress on the development of the employee engagement survey and initial findings that can enhance talent management.

☐ Launch the employee engagement survey.

Week 9: Financial Reviews:

- ☐ Collaborate with finance leaders, department heads, and executive leadership, to gain insights into financial priorities, challenges, and opportunities for cost savings.

    - ☐ Initiate financial reviews to assess the alignment of HR initiatives with budgetary constraints and explore opportunities for cost optimization.

    - ☐ Review HR budgets, departmental budgets, and overall organizational budgets, to understand current spending allocations and financial constraints.

    - ☐ Analyze the history of HR spending patterns to identify areas of significant expenditure, such as recruitment, training, benefits, and compensation.

    - ☐ Identify the main cost drivers with HR operations and initiatives.

    - ☐ Assess the return on investment (ROI) of existing HR initiatives and programs. Determine effectiveness in achieving strategic objectives.

    - ☐ Explore cost optimization strategies, such as streamlining processes, renegotiating vendor contracts, leveraging technology for efficiency gains, etc.

    - ☐ Identify quick wins for cost optimization.

- ☐ Prioritize quick wins based on impact, strategic alignment, and feasibility of implementation.

- ☐ Develop an action plan outlining these initiatives to track progress and measure success.

Third Month – Hall of Fame Mindset and Offensive Strategy Execution

Week 10: Collaborative Partnerships:

- ☐ Initiate collaborative sessions with department heads and team leaders to gather input on potential HR interventions.

- ☐ Initiate regular communication channels to foster collaboration.

- ☐ Conduct a needs assessment or facilitate focus groups to gather specific insights, requirements, goals, and key pain points.

- ☐ Prepare for your bi-weekly progress review with the CEO. Discuss progress to date and gain key insights from the CEO on the current state of the company.

Week 11: Training and Development Initiatives:

- ☐ Conduct a bi-weekly progress review with the CEO. Review your progress to date, key initiatives that you have planned for the coming weeks, and the progress of the employee engagement survey.

- ☐ Begin analysis of the employee engagement survey.

- ☐ Conduct a comprehensive assessment of training needs across the organization.

- ☐ Identify specific skills and/or competencies needed to support the current employee base.

- ☐ Once you have identified needs, define clear objectives and goals for improving existing training and development programs.

- ☐ Develop a roadmap for revitalizing training and development programs. Explore opportunities for partnerships with external training providers.

Week 12: Site Visits:

- ☐ Conduct site visits to geographically dispersed offices.

    - ☐ Assess the physical work environment, including office layout, facilities, equipment, and resources available.

    - ☐ Observe the dynamics within the teams, including communication patterns, collaboration processes, and interpersonal relationships.

    - ☐ Meet with as many employees as you can. Guage the level of employee engagement and satisfaction by gathering feedback.

    - ☐ Identify the challenges and opportunities faced by employees in their day-to-day work. Understand the nature of their work tasks, projects, and goals, as well as any obstacles or barriers they encounter.

    - ☐ Assess any training and development needs to support professional growth and skill enhancement.

    - ☐ Prepare for bi-weekly meetings with the CEO and plan to review employee engagement results.

Week 13: Prepare For the Next Game

- ☐ Facilitate the bi-weekly progress review with the CEO. Review employee engagement results and findings from site visits. Additionally, provide a recap of all findings from the first three months and discuss your plan for preparing for the next 9 months.

Having completed the first 3-month plan, you've diligently assessed the key components of the human resources function and likely identified more than you had planned.

Through this analysis, you've identified areas of strength, as well as opportunities for improvement. As you transition into the next phase, or prepare for the next game, it's imperative to maintain the momentum you've built and capitalize on the insights garnered from your assessments.

By acting decisively on key findings and leveraging your strengths, you can continue to add significant value to the organization and drive sustainable growth and success.

CONCLUSION

Celebrating a Year of Strategic Leadership

As the referee sounds the whistle for the final chapter of The 365 CHRO, it's time to reflect on the transformative journey. This playbook, inspired by the sport of football, was intended to provide strategic and tactical guidance for CHROs to support with leadership, strategic planning, and tactical execution. A few takeaways:

1. Celebrating Milestones

In the spirit of a touchdown celebration, take a moment to celebrate the milestones achieved. Acknowledge the positive changes in HR practices, the growth of your team, and the impact on the overall organization.

2. Continuous Improvement

Embrace the spirit of continuous improvement. Reflect on the successes and challenges faced throughout the year, and apply the lessons learned to refine your strategies further. The journey doesn't end here; it evolves into a new phase of growth and innovation.

3. Defining Long-Term Objectives

Now equipped with a deeper understanding of your organization and its dynamics, define long-term objectives for HR. Outline your vision for the future, incorporating the insights gained during the transformative year.

4. Tactical Adjustments for Success

Building on the tactical adjustments made during the year, continue refining your playbook. Identify areas that require fine-tuning and adjustments to ensure ongoing success. Flexibility and adaptability remain key to sustained excellence.

5. Resource Allocation Strategies

Evaluate the allocation of resources and invest strategically in areas that yield the highest returns. Whether it's talent management, technology, or training programs, align resources with the long-term goals of the organization.

6. HR Compliance

Make friends with the Referee and ensure that your team has a focus on adherence to federal, state, and local laws and regulations governing employment practices. From anti-discrimination laws to wage and hour regulations, compliance mitigates legal risks, shielding the organization from costly fines, lawsuits, and reputational damage.

7. Developing a Comprehensive 3-month CHRO Strategic Plan

Bring the insights from each chapter together to craft a comprehensive 3-month strategic CHRO plan. This plan will serve as your guide for the next phases of leadership, aligning short-term goals with the overarching vision.

In the spirit of a successful football season, this conclusion marks the beginning of a new chapter in your journey as a CHRO. Your leadership has the power to shape not only the HR function but the entire organizational landscape.

As you continue to elevate your leadership, remember that strategic planning is not a one-time event but an ongoing commitment to excellence. The lessons learned, victories celebrated, and challenges overcome during this year will serve as the foundation for a legacy of impactful HR leadership.

ABOUT THE AUTHOR

Rob, a distinguished USAF veteran and a seasoned professional is a catalyst for transformative leadership, innovation, and continuous improvement.

Military and Professional Expertise: As a USAF VETERAN, Agile Scrum master, Lean Six Sigma Green Belt, and PROSCI-certified change management practitioner, Rob brings a unique blend of military discipline and agile methodologies to the corporate arena. His multifaceted skills, coupled with over 25 + years of experience, position him as a leader in performance improvement and strategic HR planning.

Interim CHRO and Performance Improvement Consultant: Rob's journey includes serving as an Interim CHRO, where he navigated the complexities of executive leadership in the Human Resources domain. His expertise extends to various industries, reflecting a versatile and dynamic career path.

Mentorship and Coaching: Beyond his professional achievements, Rob is a dedicated mentor and coach. His commitment to guiding others reflects a passion for developing the next generation of leaders in HR and beyond.

Authorship: In his latest, Rob presents "The 365 CHRO." This book is a testament to his mission — to provide a fundamental guide for newly appointed CHROs, empowering them to establish both strategic and tactical human resources plans.

Mission: Rob's mission is rooted in a deep-seated desire to support newly hired CHROs in their journey. His book serves as a compass, offering essential insights and strategies to navigate the complexities of the CHRO role, from Change Management to Talent Management, Communications, Recruiting, Compliance, HRIS, and the development of Employee Handbooks.

Legacy of Leadership: Rob's legacy is one of leadership, innovation, and a commitment to excellence. His impact is felt not only through his vast experience but also through his dedication to empowering others in the field of Human Resources.

Visit: www.the365CHRO.com for more information.

BIBLIOGRAPHY

Ten Hagen, J. (2012). Designing and Transforming IT Organizations: Roles, Responsibilities and Organization Structures. United Kingdom: Stationery Office.

Scott, Kim. Radical Candor: Fully Revised & Updated Edition: Be a Kick-Ass Boss Without Losing Your Humanity. United States, St. Martin's Publishing Group, 2019.

Managing Human Resources: Human Resource Management in Transition. (2013). United Kingdom: Wiley.

Armstrong, S., Mitchell, B. (2008). The Essential HR Handbook: A Quick and Handy Resource for Any Manager Or HR Professional. United States: Career Press.

Kavuncu, S. C. (2018). Practical Thoughts on Human Resources Management. United Kingdom: Author House UK.

Managing Human Resources: Personnel Management in Transition. (2009). Germany: Wiley.

Watkins, M. (2003). The First 90 Days: Critical Success Strategies for New Leaders at All Levels. United Kingdom: Harvard Business School Press.

Watkins, M. D. (n.d.). Master Your Next Move, with a New Introduction: The Essential Companion to "The First 90 Days". United States: Harvard Business Review Press.

Hargrove, R. (2011). Your First 100 Days in a New Executive Job. United States: Masterful Coaching Press.

O'Keeffe, N. (2013). Lead Your Team in Your First 100 Days. United Kingdom: Pearson Education.

L. Taylor, R. (2018). Military Leadership: In Pursuit of Excellence. Ukraine: Taylor & Francis.

Duncan, D. S. (2021). The Secret Lives of Customers: A Detective Story About Solving the Mystery of Customer Behavior. United States: Public Affairs.

Harvard Business Essentials: Business Communication. (2003). United States: Harvard Business School Press.

George, M. L. (2002). Lean Six Sigma: Combining Six Sigma Quality with Lean Production Speed. United Kingdom: McGraw-Hill Education.

Jekiel, C. M. (2017). Lean Human Resources: Redesigning HR Processes for a Culture of Continuous Improvement. United Kingdom: Taylor & Francis.

O'Keeffe, N. (2011). Your First 100 Days: How to Make Maximum Impact in Your New Leadership Role. United Kingdom: Pearson.

Eubanks, B. (2022). Artificial Intelligence for HR: Use AI to Support and Develop a Successful Workforce. United Kingdom: Kogan Page.

Werner, J. (2021). Artificial Intelligence in Human Resource Management. Opportunities for the Aviation Industry. Germany: GRIN Verlag.

Wheeler, A. R., Buckley, M. R. (2021). HR Without People? Industrial Evolution in the Age of Automation, AI, and Machine Learning. United Kingdom: Emerald Publishing Limited.

NOTES

Made in the USA
Coppell, TX
25 June 2025

51121184R00114